THE RUSSIANS AND THEIR CHURCH

THE RUSSIANS AND THEIR CHURCH

BY

NICOLAS ZERNOV, D.Phil., D.D.

THIRD EDITION

ST. VLADIMIR'S SEMINARY PRESS
Crestwood, New York 10707
1978

First published in 1945 by SPCK
Third edition 1978
St. Vladimir's Seminary Press
Crestwood, New York 10707

Printed in Great Britain

ISBN 0-913836-36-2

CONTENTS

ACKNOWLEDGEMENT

The author is most grateful to E. M. Snodgrass for her help in preparing the revised edition of this book.

PREFACE TO THE 1978 EDITION

In March 1921 our family after many adventures landed at Constantinople. We had escaped the Red Terror and Communist tyranny. This was the beginning of our life in exile; we were penniless but free. Ten years later I was writing my thesis as a postgraduate student in Oxford. In 1932, after receiving my degree of Doctor of Philosophy in church history, I worked for twelve years as lecturer and organiser for the Russian Church Aid Fund and as secretary of the Fellowship of St Alban and St Sergius, a society the aim of which is to promote mutual understanding and co-operation between the Eastern and Western Christians. During those years I crossed and recrossed England and Scotland countless times, preached in churches, lectured at colleges and universities, addressed all kinds of meetings. I found many friends of Russian Christians who were keen to assist them, but at the same time I was faced by almost total ignorance of the Russian Church. There was obviously a great need of literature on this subject. The S.P.C.K. published several of my books including *The Russians and Their Church*.

In 1947 I was elected by Oxford University as Spalding Lecturer in Eastern Orthodox Culture. This appointment considerably enlarged the field of my activities and I taught and lectured in many parts of the world including the U.S.A., Canada, India and Australia. Everywhere I found the same lack of suitable information about Russian Orthodoxy. During the last two decades however the present position of the Church under Communist rule has attracted wide publicity from press, radio and television. Several excellent studies on Marxism and Christianity have also appeared in articles and books. But the background of Russian Christianity still receives much less attention. Yet its importance is evident: contemporary events spring from the past. The comprehensive history of the Russian Church still awaits its author. The fresh edition of *The Russians and Their Church* is an introduction to this vast and complex subject. It contains an additional chapter on the Russian Church during and after the second world war, a revised version of chapter XX and a new bibliography.

This book has been written in the hope that it will help to create closer links between Russian and Western Christians and to pave the way to that Christian unity which is so vital to humanity in all its present predicaments.   It is dedicated to all the friends of the Russian Christians, especially to the members of the Fellowship of St. Alban and St. Sergius[1] who during all the years of persecution in Russia worked and prayed for the reconciliation of divided Christendom.

NICOLAS ZERNOV
Ascension Day 1977
Oxford

---

[1] Further information about the Fellowship can be obtained from the Secretary at St. Basil's House, 52 Ladbroke Grove, London W11 2PB.

INTRODUCTION

The nineteenth century was the most optimistic era in history. Hitherto man had found nature incomprehensible and hostile; he was menaced by famine, pestilence and sudden death. Nor was he reassured by religion, for he was bowed before the wrath of God and fearful of the Last Judgement. In the nineteenth century all this changed. Western man at last felt his own master and at home here on earth. He saw God as a constitutional monarch firmly restricted by the laws of nature. Man learned to read these laws and found them written in his favour. He pictured himself as a rational and law-abiding being and he foresaw for himself and his successors a bright future. The climax of this optimism was reached by Karl Marx and Friedrich Engels who confidently predicted the early coming of the earthly paradise. The first world war undermined but did not destroy this faith in progress. Western man confidently began to repair the damage suffered by modern civilisation.

Few people realised the full significance of the events that took place in remote Russia, where in 1917 a new order was born which radically altered the course of history. This was totalitarianism. It was to engulf a large part of mankind and to bring about such an oppression and degradation of man as was unthinkable in the nineteenth century.

The second world war and the atomic bomb forced the West to face the grim reality of the new situation. Though the popular press and the Communistic propaganda continue to fool the masses with the promises of ever-increasing prosperity and security, it is evident that the nineteenth-century optimism is now everywhere in ruins and that man finds his very survival threatened.

The Russian people have not only initiated the new epoch of violence and compulsion, they have also been its main victims. It was they who created the Gulag Archipelago in their own land. Who are these people? What are their characteristics? Why have they inflicted upon the world the threat of Communist domination?

A nation can be best understood in the light of the three main factors which shape its character; these are the geography of the land it inhabits, the history it has experienced and the religion it has embraced. Russians differ from other people in that they are both European and Asiatic and form a link between these two worlds. This double allegiance is reflected in their history and religion; their spiritual life has been thereby enriched and at the same time exposed to tensions and conflicts. Here lies the enigma of Russia.

The secret of Russian culture is that it is both Christian and non-Western. Russians follow the Byzantine version of Eastern Orthodoxy, which is neither Roman nor Reformed. This fact has greatly contributed to the difficulty in understanding the role of the Russian Church in the evolution of the nation. This role has been at times decisive.

The difficulty is further increased by the strange silence of the Russian Church itself. Russians have always preferred to express their religious convictions through painting, music, architecture and the ritual of daily life, rather than in the written word. For long periods they were isolated from the rest of Christendom. They seldom met representatives of other confessions and consequently have not been involved in controversy with them.

The lonely road pursued by the Russian Christians came to an end in the eighteenth century. The renewed contacts with the West made the Russian Church a more articulate body; the level of scholarship was raised; theological schools were introduced; but the study of its history was still handicapped by the loss of church independence and by State censorship. Under the Communists any reference to the Church could be only negative.

Yet the study of Russian Orthodoxy is essential. It is, despite its peculiarities, an organic part of the Church Universal. The Russian Christians have been confronted by the same problems as faced others; they too have been preoccupied by the central question of how to live a Christian life under ever-changing political and social conditions; of how to be at the same time a loyal citizen and a dedicated member of the eucharistic community; of where to draw the line between Church and State. If the Russians have never yet solved this problem satisfactorily, neither have the Roman Catholics, nor Anglicans, nor Protestants. The present clash between Leninism and Christianity is the most acute stage in this perennial conflict. The religious struggle in Russia is not a local event. The confrontation between the freedom of Christian man and the tyranny of the totalitarian State has a direct bearing on the destiny of all mankind.

CHAPTER I

THE FIRST-FRUITS OF RUSSIAN CHRISTIANITY

THE Russian people were Christianised at the end of the tenth century (988). This happened some seven hundred years later than the beginning of the Church in the British Isles. It was Prince Vladimir of Kiev (d. 1015) who was responsible for the change of religion among his people. He himself invited the missionaries from the Crimea, and thus laid the foundation of the Russian Church which at first included both Eastern and Western elements of the Christian tradition.

Russia in the tenth century formed a vital link between Europe and Asia. Such rivers as the Dnieper and the Volga, and numerous lakes, provided safe water-ways for international trade; Greek, Arab, Frankish and Scandinavian merchants flocked to her big cities—Kiev in the south and Novgorod in the north. Through this miscellaneous crowd, the Russians became familiar with the great religions of the world: the Arabs were Mahometans; the Eastern neighbours of the Russians, the Khazars, professed Judaism; the Greeks belonged to the Eastern Orthodox Church; the Franks and the Scandinavians were Latin Christians. The early Russian chronicle says that Prince Vladimir, after consulting the wisest men of his land, decided to join the Eastern Orthodox Church, for he believed it best suited the temperament of his people. The Byzantine tradition of Christianity is not so institutional as the Western. It pays less attention to discipline and order but it exults in the beauty of worship and emphasises divine mercy and forgiveness.

The Russians have always been an artistic race; they find it easier to express their thoughts and feelings through music, colour, and design than through books and learned discourses. Prince Vladimir, therefore, made the right choice when he embraced the Eastern tradition. The Russians eagerly accepted their new religion, and soon felt quite at home in the brightly coloured churches which sprang up on their great open plain.

Their own pagan background, which contained many features congenial to Eastern Orthodoxy, helped the Slavs to achieve the transition without much inner struggle. The Russians before their conversion had neither temples nor an organised priesthood; they worshipped divine power revealing itself through the various manifestations of nature. The sun, the wind, the earth, and especially the thunderstorm, were considered by them to be the vehicles of divinity. The Russians possessed a keen sense of communion with the departed and held sacramental meals (called " trisna ") on the tombs of their ancestors; they also believed in benevolent and malignant spirits which inhabited woods, fields, rivers and houses. Men and women were treated by the Slavs as equals, and their social organisation consisted of small self-governing communities.

Another factor which has no parallel in the history of other nations in Europe also greatly assisted the rapid advance of Christianity among the Russians. This was the all-important fact that they heard the Gospel preached and the services celebrated in the vernacular, and this from the very beginning of their Christian history. Most of the Western nations had been kept by the Church for many centuries in the school of Latin learning. It was a salutary, though sometimes rigid, training, which helped the people of Europe to appreciate logic and discipline and created a bond of unity among them. The Russians have not participated in this experience. They were also brought into the fellowship of the Christian Church, but through a special door, and therefore they remained a peculiar member, differing in many ways from the rest of the body. The Russians shared with other Christians the Bible, the Creed, the threefold ministry, and parish organisation. They took the ritual from Byzantium and were profoundly influenced by its beauty and artistic perfection.

But having in common with others the fundamental elements of their newly acquired religion, the Russians found their own approach to it. The majority of Christians saw the Church in the light of the Greek and Latin theological writings. The Russians were the only people in Europe who remained outside this influence; and this made it possible for them to understand Christianity in their own way.

Their attitude to religion was much less philosophical than the Byzantine, and much less institutional than the Latin. It might perhaps appear too direct and too spontaneous to other more learned and sophisticated Christians, but it contained new and deep insight into Christian truth and stressed a side of Church life which was neglected by other traditions.

Prince Vladimir was the first to display the typically Russian interpretation of Christianity. Before his conversion, this bellicose Prince had little idea of restraint or self-control. He was bold in battle, fond of food and drink, had several wives and a large number of children. His baptism radically changed his behaviour, but he did not become morose and retiring; on the contrary, he discovered a new joy in life, and directed his strong and generous nature towards helping the orphaned, the poor, and the sick. His Court retained its fame for the banquets of his heathen days, but, instead of inviting the powerful and the rich, he opened his gates to the hungry and the afflicted. He built homes for the aged and for invalids. Especially striking was his attitude to criminals: this man, who had previously shed blood liberally in fierce battles, realised the sacredness of each human life, and his first impulse was to abolish capital punishment in his vast dominion. This decision greatly surprised the clergy whom he had brought from the Crimea. The Byzantine Empire inherited from its pagan days a system of cruel punishments. Though it was considerably humanised under Christian influence, it nevertheless retained tortures and mutilations for the guilty. The Greek bishops, used to this type of legislation, when consulted by Vladimir, advised the newly converted Prince not to relax the laws against evil-doers; they insisted that the ruler had a duty to punish the wicked severely. Prince Vladimir reluctantly obeyed, but he did not change his mind and remained convinced that tortures and capital punishment had no place in a Christian community. This opinion has been maintained by a large number of Russian Christians, and several outstanding rulers—such as Prince Vladimir Monomakh (*d.* 1125), the Empress Elizabeth (*d.* 1761), and Alexander II (*d.* 1881)—won universal approval by banishing capital punishment from the legislation of the land. The belief that law-breakers ought to be treated as unfortunate victims of their own and others' sins, rather than as persons deserving exemplary retribution, has always been widespread among Russian Christians.[1] Equally typical of their outlook has been that generosity to the poor which was first displayed by Vladimir, and which often appears

[1] In colloquial Russian " unfortunate " is often used instead of the word " criminal."

extravagant to foreign observers trained in the more reserved
atmosphere of the West.

The unusual circumstances, in which Vladimir's two youngest
sons lost their lives, serve as another illustration of the peculiarly
Russian approach to religion. Vladimir had eleven sons, and,
after his death, the eldest of them, Sviatopolk, made an attempt
to get rid of his brothers and to become the sole ruler of the
country. He chose as the first object of his attack one of them,
Prince Boris, who was not yet twenty. Boris was at the head
of a strong detachment of his father's troops when he learned
about the hostile designs of his half-brother. Though only a
youth, he was popular among his men and had already acquired
a reputation as a skilful leader in defending the country against
nomads. Yet instead of resisting Sviatopolk he gave up the fight
and was pitilessly murdered. His contemporary biographer
describes his last day as spent in grief and lamentation. He was
in the prime of his youth and he wanted to live, but as a Christian he felt that he was not justified in bringing about the death
of others in defence of his own life. He was prepared to lead
his men into battle when they were protecting their families and
homes against barbaric intruders, but this time the situation was
different, for this enemy wanted only his destruction. Boris
decided to sacrifice his life in order to follow Christ's example by
accepting an innocent suffering and death.

His brother, Gleb, followed his example and perished a few
days later in similar circumstances.

The Russian people were profoundly stirred by the conduct of
the young princes. Their behaviour had no precedent in the
history of the Church. The bishops, sent to Russia from Byzantium, thought the action of the two youths was foolish, but such
was not the verdict of the Russians themselves. They declared
that the voluntary death of the brothers was a genuine Christian
action, a fulfilment of Christ's commandment to resist evil by
good. The hierarchs, under pressure of public opinion, had to
give up their opposition, and Boris and Gleb were the first Saints
canonised by the Russian Church (1020). They remain till
the present time among the most beloved members of the Christian
family of the Russian people, and their example never fails to
excite warm admiration. Boris and Gleb were not called martyrs, for they did not die in defence of their faith; they are called
instead by the name of " Passion-Bearers ", which emphasises the

novelty of their interpretation of what Christian conduct ought to be.

The story of Boris and Gleb shows that the seeds of the Christian religion fell on fertile soil in Russia, and that the nation accepted wholeheartedly the new teaching. It also reveals that Christianity was understood by Russian people neither as a system of doctrines nor as an institution, but primarily as a way of life. The same approach is further illustrated by the peculiar character of early Russian Monasticism. Its founder, St. Theodosius (d. 1074), laid great stress on the social work of the monks, and his famous Monastery of the Caves, near Kiev, became an example of true brotherhood and of generous help to those in distress. Theodosius himself took an active interest in public affairs, and his interventions in the disputes of the Princes saved Russia several times from civil war. The tradition started by him was followed by other Russian monks. They were ready to assist lay people not only in their spiritual problems, but also in their material concerns, believing that the whole of man's life must be illuminated by the light of the Gospel.

The high level of Christian conduct reached by the enlightened section of Russian society is also revealed by Vladimir Monomakh (d. 1125), the most outstanding ruler of the Kiev period of Russian history. He was a man of many gifts. One of the best educated Princes of that time in Europe, he was endowed with exceptional mental and physical energy. He was tireless in the exercise of his princely duties, courageous on the battlefield, wise and merciful in administering justice, generous to the poor, a patron of art and learning. He was a devout Christian and followed Christ in the perplexing and difficult circumstances created by his manifold responsibilities. For example, when one of his sons was killed by another prince, instead of avenging his son's death, according to the custom of his time, he himself took the first step towards reconciliation, for he recognised that his son was the guilty party in the quarrel. His moral authority stood so high that other Russian princes willingly followed his lead, and he several times convoked conferences at which questions of general policy were discussed and settled in the spirit of equality and justice. His philosophy of life has been preserved through his own writing, entitled " A Charge to my Children ". After describing various adventures of his successful career, he enumerates the principles which he chose for the guidance of his conduct. He wrote: "My children, praise God, and love men. For it is not fasting, nor solitude, nor monastic life that will procure you eternal life, but only doing good. Forget not the poor, but feed them. Remember that riches come from God and are given you only for a short time. Do not bury your wealth in the ground; this is against the precepts of Christianity.[1] Be fathers to orphans, be judges in the cause of widows and do not let the powerful oppress the weak. Put to death neither the innocent nor the guilty, for nothing is so sacred as the life and the soul of a Christian.[2] Do not desert the sick; do not let the sight of corpses terrify you, for we must all die. Drive out of your heart all suggestions of pride and remember that we are all mortal, to-day full of hope, to-morrow in the coffin. Abhor lying, drunkenness and debauchery. Endeavour constantly to obtain knowledge. Without having quitted his country, my father learned five foreign languages, a thing which won for him the admiration of foreigners." [3]

Prince Vladimir stood above his contemporaries but not outside their ranks. His "charge" enjoyed great esteem and remained favourite reading for several generations. He expressed ideals universally shared by Russian Christians, and his authority was high because he not only taught well but also behaved in accordance with his teaching.

The period of prosperity and commercial and cultural links with the rest of Christendom enjoyed by the Russians of the Kiev period did not last long, however, and soon a marked decline set in, caused by the collapse of their political order.

[1] He is referring to a pagan custom of burying the bodies of the wealthy with their most valuable possessions.

[2] This is another example of a typically Russian repudiation of capital punishment in a State which claims to be Christian.

[3] The knowledge of foreign languages was one of the marks of the high level of Russian culture in the eleventh and twelfth centuries. At the time when King John of England could only put a cross under Magna Carta, a Russian prince could speak Greek and Latin as well as he spoke Russian. This is a statement made by the chronicler, for instance, about Prince Michael, grandson of Vladimir Monomakh.

CHAPTER II

THE CHURCH AND THE GROWTH OF
RUSSIAN CULTURE

THE culture and wealth of Russia, and especially that of her big
cities, depended on international trade. As long as this flourished, Kiev retained the rank of one of the greatest cities in
Europe, and its princes were known and respected in all parts of
the world. There was hardly any Royal house in the twelfth
century, in France, England, Germany, or Scandinavia, which
was not connected, by marriage, with Russia's ruling family, the
House of Rurik.

Some idea of the size of the Russian capital is given by the
figure of six hundred churches destroyed there by the great fire
of 1124. It is no wonder, therefore, that contemporary writers
compare Kiev favourably even with Constantinople, the Imperial
city of the Christian East.

The basis of Russian prosperity proved, however, to be of an
unstable character. In the second part of the twelfth century,
owing to the Crusaders and to other causes beyond Russian
control, the flow of commerce between Europe and Asia was
directed away from the Russian water-ways, and this provoked
a rapid decline of the previously flourishing cities. This adversity
was further aggravated by the renewal of fierce attacks by the
nomads from the Steppes upon the wealthy but poorly protected
Russian settlements and by the increase of rivalries and hostility
among the Russian princes.

The strength and the weakness of the Russians have always
been their tendency to treat their nation as one big family. This
offered to men like Vladimir Monomakh a wide opportunity to
exercise moral influence over the whole nation and gave to all
Russians a sense of belonging to the same body. But it had also
some serious disadvantages. The chief among them was the
confusion between private and State interests, which led to chaos
in the administration of the country. The Russia of the Kiev
period was neither one State with a centralised form of government nor a federation of independent principalities. It was a
curious country, inhabited by different nationalities and races,

11

containing a number of self-governing cities, and yet ruled by one family, the House of Rurik. Each prince belonging to it had a share in the administration of the land, and his seniority in the family determined the degree of his importance.

The eldest representative of the House of Rurik had his seat in the capital, in Kiev. He was supposed to look after the welfare of the whole land and to co-ordinate the activities of other princes, especially in time of external danger, when common action was required. He was, however, only a first among equals, for others had their own seats in cities and towns, though the younger they were the less important was the centre allotted to them. When the Grand Prince of Kiev died, his seat was taken not by his son, but by his brother. This meant a move for all the other princes, for each of them mounted a step higher, exchanging a lesser for a bigger town. The princes were not autocrats; they were primarily the military defenders of their cities, and also the supreme judges, but the regular administration of a city was in the hands of the local Councils elected by the people's Assembly.

Russian life during the Kiev period was centred in towns, inhabited by enterprising and freedom-loving citizens, who were jealous of their traditional liberties, and any prince who infringed these was in danger of being expelled from his seat by the populace. The system of government evolved during that period favoured local autonomy, and yet it kept the whole vast country closely knit together, for the princes, accompanied by their bodyguards and retinues, moved constantly from one place to another and thus maintained intercourse between the remotest corners of the Russian land. There was, however, one serious defect in this order, and that was the insufficiency of power given to the Grand Prince. Instead of equipping him with political and military weapons, strong enough to enable him to secure obedience, the Russians ascribed to him only moral authority. The smooth working of this complicated form of government depended therefore on the personal quality of the Grand Prince. When the seat of Kiev was occupied by such men as Vladimir Monomakh (*d.* 1125), his father Vsevolod (*d.* 1093), or Mstislav I (*d.* 1132), peace reigned in the country, for they commanded respect and could make princes and cities follow their lead without resorting to compulsion. These were, however, exceptional personalities, and they do not therefore disprove the general rule that every political system needs for its stability both moral authority and sufficient force for use against law-breakers. The last condition was neglected by the Russians. The Grand Prince was not a ruler whom the rest of the princes had to obey. All of them enjoyed the right to oppose the Prince of Kiev if they believed him to be wrong. Disputes were inevitable; these led to military clashes, and military clashes brought with them civil war, with its plunder of the defeated, burning of towns and villages, and suffering for the common people.

From the middle of the twelfth century, Russia knew no peace. Her princes became engaged in a never-ending struggle in which the notion of proper succession became utterly confused, and the stronger and more audacious members of Rurik's family began to seize by force the more prosperous towns and hold them till they were ejected by those rivals who had a still stronger army. Kiev, the capital, was the centre of a particularly bitter struggle. During the twenty-three years from 1146 till 1169, it was held by twelve different princes, and only one of them was able to remain in power for as long as six years. In these years of anarchy and political decline, the only force that cared equally for all Russians was the Church. There was a striking contrast between the breakdown of the political system and the steady growth of the Christian religion among the Russians. The leadership in the State was in the hands of the princes; they were all members of the same family, but they were actuated by rivalry and hostility. The leaders of the Church were recruited from the most diverse sections of Russian society, but, though they had no ties of blood, they lived in unity, for they were all animated by the same Spirit.

The Russian Church was the daughter of the Church of the Byzantine Empire, but the general conditions of the country were so different that its function was considerably modified in Russia in comparison with its manner of working in the land of its origin. This was particularly marked in the relation between Church and State. In the Byzantine Empire, the State was well-established and was supreme. Only after a hard struggle, and when its leaders had realised that they could not destroy the Church, had they accorded to it a recognised place. Church and State remained two clearly defined bodies; their relations were governed by canon law, and the Emperor, who exercised supreme control over all the activities of his subjects, dealt with State matters through the medium of the Senate, and with ecclesiastical matters through the medium of the Oecumenical Councils summoned by him from time to time. The Patriarch of Constantinople, as the senior hierarch of the Eastern Empire, acted as a permanent link between the Emperor and the Church in the intervals between Councils. The foundations of the Empire remained pagan, and the Emperor was still treated as a superhuman being. The gorgeous ceremonies of the Court reflected the pride and vainglory of the Roman State. Christian influence had little chance of penetrating into this stronghold of ancient paganism. The Church had, however, the power to change the life of its members, and thus a gulf was created between the moral aspirations of individuals and the general social and political conditions of the Empire. Many of the best Christians were not able to face these contradictions, and they joined religious communities or fled into the desert in search of an integral Christian life.

The heathen Empire officially ceased to exist at the time of Constantine's conversion in the fourth century, but it was not really destroyed: it tenaciously resisted the spirit of Christian brotherhood, freedom, and forgiveness, and, under cover of religious orthodoxy, maintained its Roman idea of the State.

The situation in Russia was quite different. The nation had no traditions which could compete with Christianity. When the Russians were brought into the fellowship of the Orthodox Church, they were introduced into the superior world of Mediterranean civilisation. The level of its culture and its artistic achievements were far above those reached by the Russians themselves, but the inhabitants of the Eastern Empire were, on the other hand, victims of such vice, cruelty, and superstitition as were unknown to the childlike Slavonic peoples. Fortunately, however, the channel of communication between teacher and pupil was so restricted by distance and by Russian ignorance of the Greek language, that the bulk of the Slavs became familiar with the spiritual treasures of the Orthodox Church without being seriously affected by the negative features of the great Eastern realm.

The Slavonic translation of the New Testament, the Psalms, the Service Books, a few writings of the Fathers, and, above all, the Eucharistic Liturgy, were the main gifts brought to the Russians by their Church, and on these foundations they built up their culture. The Church in Russia had an open field for action, and though its resources were more limited than in other countries, its members made good use of them.

The mainspring of its life was the parish church where, contrary to Western practice, a prominent part in the worship was played by the lay people. The clergy in Russia occupied a less conspicuous place in the services than they did in the Latin and, later, in the Reformed Churches. There were no pulpits, and a priest never dominated his congregation; he took his position behind the screen, being neither much seen nor much heard by his people. The major portion of the offices was sung or read by the laity. They formed the mixed choirs, they filled the nave of the church, they were inspired by the moving words of the prayers and hymns and by the religious paintings, which covered the screen, the walls, and the ceilings of church buildings and provided instruction suitable even for the illiterate and least educated of the congregation.

The church was for a Russian his university, his theatre, his concert-hall and his picture-gallery. On Sundays and feast days, the entire population gathered for the celebration of the Eucharist. The people listened to the reading of the Scriptures; they recited the Psalms and the Creed, lamented over Christ's sufferings and death and rejoiced in His Resurrection and Ascension. This was a unique training ground for them, which enlightened their hearts and minds and introduced them to the mystery of Divine Redemption.

Close to the parish church stood a school, an almshouse, and dwellings for the clergy. Several times a year, all the parishioners had a common meal near the church, as an expression of their equality and brotherhood. The clergy—priests, deacons, readers and choirmasters, and other minor officials—were all elected by their parishioners and were supported by their voluntary contributions. They were a large body and were exempt from ordinary legislation, for they lived under their own ecclesiastical law. This latter was copied from the Byzantine codes but was made more humane by the Russian translators. This code, known under the name of " Kozmchaia Kniga ", had a wide influence upon all spheres of Russian life. By its means the Church taught people higher ideas of justice, fairer treatment of the defenceless, forgiveness instead of vengeance. Not only all the clergy, but also doctors, nurses, orphans, widows, and all outcasts had the right to be judged by this code. Family disputes, ques-

tions of divorce, women's rights to property, daughters' shares
in inheritance, were also subjected to the ecclesiastical courts,
for a woman enjoyed the special protection of the Church.

Besides parishes, Russian Christian life had its vital centres in
monasteries and convents. From these the people learned the art
of prayer, self-denial and charity. The bishops were mostly
recruited from among the monks, who were better trained than
the parish clergy. Missionary work also occupied an important
place in the various activities of the Church. The task of
evangelisation was difficult only among the Finnish tribes.
These stubbornly clung to their paganism and actively resisted
those who tried to convert them to the new religion. Several
missionaries lost their lives whilst preaching the Gospel in the
eastern province of the country where the Finns predominated.
In spite of this opposition and sporadic acts of violence, Christianity spread rapidly all over the country; it was not imposed
by force, and this peaceful penetration contributed to its strong
hold on the people's life. By the end of the eleventh century,
Russia was a distinctly Christian country, and not only the
cities but even remote villages were firmly won to Christianity.

The higher forms of ecclesiastical organisation remained
undeveloped, however, for many centuries to come. The Bishop
of Kiev bore the title of Metropolitan; he was appointed by
the Patriarch of Constantinople and with few exceptions was a
Greek.[1] He had the right of confirming the bishops in their
office, but he had no effective control over the rest of the episcopate and no real Metropolitan authority. As the cities and princes
tenaciously clung to their independence, so the bishops objected
to Metropolitan interference in the affairs of their dioceses. The
latter coincided with the frontiers of the chief principalities, and
were so enormous that each of them would have been treated
as a Metropolitan Province in Greece or Italy.

---

[1] There is strong evidence that the Russian Church was at first independent
of Constantinople. Prince Vladimir favoured the idea of a Church which
would combine both Eastern and Western characteristics and remain self-
governing. This policy was revised by his son Iaroslav the Wise (1019–54),
who submitted his Church to Constantinople. This victory of the pro-Byzan-
tine party was marked by the building of a second cathedral in Kiev, dedicated
this time to St. Sophia. It was consecrated in 1039 by the Greek Bishop
Theopemptous (1039–54), who was sent from Constantinople. See N. Zernov,
" Prince Vladimir and the origin of the Russian Church ", Slavonic Review,
Nov. 1949, April 1950.

The bishops took an active part in the civic life of their flock. In the unstable conditions of the country, they had often greater influence than the princes, for they represented the interests of the whole community, whilst a prince was often a partisan of his own cause. This was particularly true in such cities as Novgorod or Pskov, where princes were constantly changing and the only authority recognised by the populace of these commercial centres was that of their bishops.

The entire culture of Russia during the Kiev period of its history (from the ninth to the thirteenth century) was inspired and guided by the Orthodox Church. The few monuments of its art that have survived the Tartar invasion all display a high level. Russian architecture, påinting, embroidery, poetry, social customs and legislation could be favourably compared with the achievements of any other Christian nation of that time, but in the sphere of politics the Russians were not so successful. They failed to create a stable order, and this had fatal consequences for them at the tragic hour which struck in the middle of the thirteenth century, when their country was suddenly invaded by the Tartars.

CHAPTER III

THE TARTARS AND PRINCE ALEXANDER NEVSKI

THE world-wide conquest started by the Tartars at the beginning of the thirteenth century was the last and most devastating of the waves of invasion which the unknown steppes of Central Asia from time immemorial had sent out to the neighbouring countries. These waves brought with them destruction, slavery and death. In the thirteenth century, once more, millions of human beings perished in this unequal struggle.

The Tartars were a branch of the Mongols, and they inhabited the Altai region of Siberia. Split into many tribes, which were always quarrelling with one another, the Mongols, before this period, had been weak and despised by their neighbours. No one could imagine them as a master race, yet they became the builders of one of the greatest Empires of the world. This sudden transformation was the work of a single man known under the name of Chingiz Khan (1155–1227). He succeeded in uniting all the Mongols and in welding them into a compact and efficient war machine, which he, with supreme skill, used for the defeat and annihilation of other States and nations. Central Asia, China, Turkestan, Persia, Asia Minor, Russia, Central and Southern Europe and, later on, India, were, one after the other, devastated by the Tartars. As far as Europe was concerned, the Tartar invasion was a temporary calamity, but for the rest of Asia and for Russia the Mongol assault was followed by a long period of subjugation to the nomadic conquerors. The face of all these lands was radically changed, and Russian history is sharply divided into two periods, before and after the Tartar invasion.

The first appearance of the Tartars in the southern steppes occurred in 1223. Like lightning they struck, inflicting a crushing defeat upon the coalition of Russian princes. Then, instead of pursuing the remnants of the Russian army, the Tartars rapidly withdrew into the depths of Asia, leaving the Russians in complete bewilderment. No one in Russia had ever heard of them before, and no one knew whence they came, nor whither they had gone. Several years passed in peace, and the Russians began to hope that they would not again meet the Tartars. These hopes proved false. The Tartars reappeared fifteen years later. This time, they came with the intention of making Russia part of their pan-Asiatic Empire. In November 1237, Khan Batu (d. 1255), the grandson of Chingiz Khan, at the head of 400,000 horsemen, invaded Russia. This formidable army, at that time the best in the world, was larger than all the military forces at the disposal of the Russians. The command of the Tartars was highly centralised; they had a master-plan for conquest and they acted swiftly and resolutely. The Russians were split into many independent principalities; they had no knowledge of their enemy and no plan for the defence of their country. The fate of the nation was sealed before the battle began. The Russians fought with supreme courage, but they were everywhere outnumbered and outmanœuvred, and by the end of 1240 Russia had ceased to exist as an independent State. The land suffered a terrifying devastation. The Tartars did not fight only the armed forces of their enemies; their aim was the destruction of the entire population. Whenever a town or village was taken, all the houses were burnt down, all the people were massacred or carried away as slaves. Wherever the Tartars passed, only corpses and charred ruins were left behind.

The Papal envoy John of Piano Carpini, travelled to the Court of the Mongol Khans soon after the fatal blow occurred in 1246. He records that when he entered Russian territory he did not come across any towns or villages, but saw only countless human skulls and the looted remnants of once flourishing cities. Kiev and its fertile plain suffered most, and for the next two hundred years remained a scene of desolation.

Yet the Tartars failed to destroy Russia. Deeply humiliated, severely wounded, the nation refused to die. With stubborn resolution, the people began to rebuild their land. The central regions of Russia were destroyed beyond immediate repair, but conditions were more favourable on the fringes of the country. In the next two centuries, Russian life became split into three parts, each of which showed its distinct characteristics. These were the south-western provinces of Galicia and Volhynia; the north-western corner dominated by the city republics of Novgorod and Pskov; and the north-eastern woodlands with their chief towns of Vladimir, Rostov, Iaroslavl, and Susdal. All these parts of the country were better sheltered, geographically, from

the fury of the nomads, than Kiev and the neighbouring steppes—
Galicia and Volhynia were close to the Carpathians; the north-
west corner was surrounded by the marshes, and the north-east
had the excellent protection of immense forests.

The fact that in these three regions the population escaped
the wholesale destruction that befell those who lived in the open
plains of the south made possible the physical revival of the
nation, but the spirit needed for such revival was provided by
the Russian Church, and pre-eminently by its outstanding representatives, such as Prince Alexander Nevski, the Metropolitans
Cyril, Peter and Alexis, and St. Sergius of Radonezh.

The chance of recovery for the Russian people was also
increased by the Tartars' desire to secure an income from
the conquered territories. As soon as the horrors of massacre
were over, they turned from fierce ravagers into thrifty owners.
They became interested in the resumption of normal activities
among the remnants of the broken nation. Those Russians who
survived were allowed to rebuild their towns and resume their
work, though no longer as free people, but as the slaves of their
new masters. In order to facilitate administration, the Tartars
reinstated the princes of the House of Rurik and ordered them
to take the responsibility for the collection of the heavy taxes
and for the maintenance of discipline among the conquered people.

The Tartars were not only first-class warriors, they were also
able rulers. Chingiz Khan employed as his civilian advisers the
experienced bureaucrats of the Chinese Empire. One of them,
Ye-liu Chu-tsai, who was a financier, a poet, a scholar and an
astronomer, was as much responsible for the success of the conquest as the great military master himself. The combination of
the wild courage and inexhaustible energy of the nomads with
the high technique of Chinese administration, evolved during
long centuries of statesmanship, produced that stable compound
which for many years to come endured the terrific pressure of
disruptive forces created by the vast expanse of the newly-
founded Empire.

The Russians found themselves faced with a hard choice.
Either they could give up the struggle as hopeless, consent to be
merged in the Mongolian world and so lose their individuality
(the fate that befell several Asiatic nations), or they could continue their open resistance, preferring death to slavery. This
last course made a strong appeal to many of the Russians.

But it would have meant national suicide, and the country was delivered from this by Alexander Nevski (*d.* 1263). He took upon his shoulders the burden of responsibility for the choice of direction in the reconstruction of national life. His courage, humility and faith gave him power to lead the people in their first steps along a narrow and dangerous path surrounded by still-smoking ruins. The path he chose was the right one, and it eventually brought Russia back to power and freedom.

Alexander was a youth of eighteen at the time of the Tartar invasion. He lived in Novgorod, and this saved him from death, for the capital of the North was one of the few cities which escaped destruction. " Lord Novgorod the Great ", as it was called by the Russians, was a rich merchant-republic in the thirteenth century. It extended its dominion over vast territories in the northern parts of the country, but it continued to invite princes of the House of Rurik to be its military governors and thus remained linked with the rest of the nation.

To be Prince of Novgorod was a precarious business, for the unruly inhabitants of the great city were always ready to expel their governor if he failed to satisfy their demands. At the same time, Novgorod was one of the leading States, and the competing branches of the Rurik family were eager to have one of their faction in control of this all-important post. Prince Iaroslav (*d.* 1246), Alexander's father, after a hard struggle, succeeded in placing his son in Novgorod (1231), and this opened to the young Prince the arduous road of service to his country in the time of its greatest calamity.

There is a Russian proverb which says, " When misfortune comes, one must open the gates wide ", for often one trouble brings with it many others. The truth of this observation was confirmed in the years which followed the Tartar invasion. As soon as the news of disaster reached Russia's western neighbours, they hastily organised a crusade. Its object, however, was not to fight against the heathen Mongols. The crusaders wanted to destroy the last two outposts of Eastern Christianity, Novgorod and Pskov, which had been spared by the nomads. This new attack came from two sides: the Swedes landed on the shores of the river Neva, whilst the Teutonic Knights, who had established their stronghold in Riga, moved eastwards, conquering and subjugating the native population.

The people of Novgorod were panic-stricken. The rest of

the country lay in ruins; they themselves could expect any day a renewal of the Tartar assault, and here was a new enemy threatening their very existence. They turned for help to their young Prince, and he had the courage to accept the challenge. He was cut off from the rest of the family. There was nobody whose advice he could ask, but he was a man of deep faith, and his biography ascribes to him the authorship of a prayer expressing his strong conviction that God rules the nations and that nothing happens against His will. This prayer contains the following sentence: " O Lord of truth and power, who dost order all nations to remain in their own dominions, and who dost fix their boundaries, look upon the plight of Thy servants, and give them strength to expel the invaders ". Inspired by confidence in the righteousness of his cause, Alexander, at the head of a small army of picked men, defeated the Swedes (1240) and, two years later, on April 5th, 1242, on the ice of the Lake of Chud, he inflicted a crushing blow upon the superior force of the heavily-armed Teutonic Knights. This victory saved Novgorod and stopped the German advance towards the east. Latin Christendom had at last met an obstacle which it failed to overcome. All that was on the western side of the battle-field came under Germanic domination, but on the eastern side the Russians remained masters of their own destiny, and their Church continued to be the spiritual leader of the people.

The threat to Russian integrity from the West was even greater than the danger from the Tartars. The nomads oppressed and ill-treated the Russians, but they had no desire to leave their cultural imprint upon the conquered nation. They were tolerant in religious matters, and they granted privileges to the Russian Church, for they revered divine power under whatever form it was worshipped. The Mongols swept across the Russian plain like a fierce flood, but they receded afterwards with similar rapidity into their own domain of the steppes. The Christian West pursued an entirely opposite policy. It moved slowly, but each time it made a new advance it established a permanent hold on the conquered territory. The crusaders aimed at the final eradication of the Eastern Orthodox tradition and at its replacement by Latin Christianity.

The brilliant victory won by the young hero on the western frontier led to a crisis in the east. The Tartars kept a careful watch over all Alexander's movements, and in 1247 he received a summons from Khan Batu, who governed Russia from his headquarters on the banks of the Volga, to come in person in order to pay homage to the overlord of the Russian land. This visit entailed a grave personal risk for the prince. The Russians still expected their early liberation, and the eyes of all were fixed on the victor over their Western enemies. This was known to the Tartars, who were suspicious of Alexander's intentions. Several Russian princes, whose loyalty to the Mongols was questioned, had failed to return from a visit to Batu, and many feared that this would be Alexander's fate.

He, however, refused to listen to those who advised him to disregard the summons, and he obediently started on the long and perilous journey. He was a man of great courage and exceptional physical strength, but at the same time he was profoundly humble, and this made him a realist. He was free from personal ambitions, his only concern was to serve the nation, he knew that the country had no power to resist the Mongols, and therefore he considered that his duty was to obey Khan Batu. His own safety and honour he was ready to sacrifice for the sake of his people. So it happened that the brilliant victor over the crusaders prostrated himself like a slave four times before the Tartar lord. Batu was a shrewd ruler. As a Mongol, he had a genuine respect for a man of courage, and he also realised the importance of the Russian prince who lay prostrate at his feet. He received him with honour but did not allow him to return home. The Khan ordered Alexander to proceed farther east, and to appear before the Supreme Ruler of all the Tartars, who supervised his immense Empire from Karakorum in Mongolia.

The road across the desert and high mountains of Turkestan and Mongolia was long and full of hardship. It took Alexander three years to complete his journey, but when he returned to Russia in 1250 with the title of Grand Prince of Kiev, he was a man with experience such as no Russian leader had ever had. Alexander saw with his own eyes the extent and strength of the new Empire. He met, in the strange city of tents, in the middle of Mongolia, men from China, India and Persia. After the simplicity of Russian life, he was struck by the splendour and variety of Asiatic customs, and he realised that these nations were kept together by the iron rule of the all-powerful Mongols. He was able to observe the working of the vast military machine organised so efficiently by the Tartars. Owing to the excellence of his communications, the Supreme Khan could put into action, at the shortest notice, vast armies in the remotest parts of his dominion.

Equipped with this knowledge, Alexander returned to his ruined country, and there he had to face the hardest task of his life. This was to teach the Russians two lessons which they were loth to learn: first, that spontaneous outbreaks of revolt, however courageous, had not the least chance of liberating the country from the Tartars; secondly, that their national independence could be secured only when they submitted to discipline and were ready to obey their own rulers. But the Russians, exasperated by the heavy taxation imposed by the Mongols and by the cruelty of the punitive expeditions, would not listen, and staged one rebellion after another. Alexander's own brother, Andrei, led one of the most audacious of them. They were all crushed by the Tartars, and Alexander had to appear several times before the Khans and implore their mercy and forgiveness.

The Tartars knew that Alexander was opposed to these desperate acts of resistance, and his interventions saved Russia from the fury of their Oriental vengeance. His policy was understood by only a few Russians; the hero of the early victories over the crusaders was accused of cowardice and indecision. Alexander had to endure unpopularity, calumny and base insinuations. Even his strong constitution was not able to stand the strain of his service to the nation. Utterly exhausted, he died on November 14th, 1263, at the early age of 42. Death overcame him on his return journey from the Tartar headquarters, after he had once more successfully fulfilled his mission and obtained a pardon—this time for the citizens of Novgorod.

Only when the Russians learned that Alexander was no longer with them, did they realise how much they owed him. A wave of spontaneous grief swept across the country. Cyril, the Metropolitan of Russia, expressed this sentiment when, on being informed of Alexander's sudden death, he interrupted the celebration of the Liturgy and said to the assembled people: "My dear children, know that the Sun of Russia has set. Prince Alexander is no longer with us." The whole congregation burst into tears.

Alexander was canonised in 1380. He was included in the list of the Saints not because he was a successful defender of the country and one of its most far-seeing rulers—national heroes have never been honoured in this way by the Russian people.

He is a Saint because he was a Christian of exceptional integrity and faith. He was able to carry the heavy cross of serving his defeated people, without pride or despair, and he remained firm and humble in spite of every kind of derision and insult.

His line of conduct was prophetic. He was in tune with the new Russia which was slowly and painfully rising from the ruins of the Tartar invasion—a Russia with profound experience of suffering and humiliation, a nation which eventually learned the lesson of unity, patience and endurance. Alexander had the moral strength to accept the grim truth that neither he nor his children would see their native land set free. He was not crushed by the knowledge that unconditional surrender to the Asiatic invaders was, for the time being, the only policy open to his people. His firm faith in God, the Ruler over all nations, gave him confidence in the remote yet certain victory of the Christians over their heathen oppressors. He stood far above his generation, and his gaze could penetrate into that distant future when once more Orthodox Russia would be master of the great Eurasian plain. But few of his contemporaries were able to share his vision. The most outstanding among his friends and supporters was the Metropolitan of Kiev, Cyril (1242–81).

Cyril was a Russian, for the Patriarch of Constantinople could not find any Greek Prelate willing to go to devastated Russia. For thirty-nine years this indefatigable man travelled all over the country, consoling and instructing his scattered flock, ordaining priests, rebuilding churches. The Mongols treated the Russian clergy and their Metropolitan with the same respect which they afforded to all ministers of religion. The clergy were the only section of the subjugated population exempt from taxation, and every act of violence inflicted upon them by any of the Tartars was punishable by death. These privileges offered great possibilities for constructive work to men of Cyril's ability and perseverance. He inaugurated a new type of service for the Metropolitans of Russia.

Before the Tartar invasion, the chief hierarchs of the Russian Church were mainly occupied with ecclesiastical matters. After the invasions, the Metropolitans became equally concerned with the national revival of the country. Their authority alone was recognised by all the people, and the esteem paid to them by the Tartars raised their prestige high above that of any of the secular rulers. But none of them made any attempt to obtain

political power.   Their policy consisted in giving moral support
to those princes who showed greater statesmanship and were
ready to work for national unity.   This conduct brought rich
reward, and established friendship and mutual trust between the
leaders of Church and State.   The subsequent liberation of the
country was primarily due to the stabilising influence of the
Church, which was able to inspire with new courage and faith the
disheartened and down-trodden people.

CHAPTER IV

THE RE-BIRTH OF THE NATION

IT often happens that the harmful effects of a disaster are not fully felt at once. Only after a lapse of time does an individual or a nation experience all the destructive consequences. This happened to the Russians in the thirteenth century. In the first decades following the onslaught of the Tartars, the nation was sustained by the hope of early liberation, and only a few far-seeing leaders, such as Alexander Nevski and the Metropolitan Cyril, were aware that long years of slavery lay ahead for the conquered people. Gradually this knowledge dawned upon the masses, and apathy, despair and cynicism spread like malignant growths, especially among the remnants of the ruling classes.

The end of the thirteenth century and the beginning of the fourteenth century were particularly dark in the history of Russia. The North-eastern Provinces, with their main cities, Vladimir, Iaroslavl, Rostov and Susdal, became the helpless prey of renewed competition among the princes, aggravated this time by the intervention of the Tartars. The brothers and sons of Alexander Nevski, with the exception of his youngest son Daniel, displayed his military valour but none of his virtues. They fought each other for the title of Grand Prince and had no scruples about asking the Tartars to help them to defeat their rivals. The Mongols gladly seized this opportunity for further plunder and massacre of the Russian people and laid waste towns and villages. The state of things in Novgorod and Pskov was no better. The citizens of these republics were split into hostile factions and constantly quarrelled among themselves. As a result, the Russians lost large slices of territory round the Baltic Sea to the Germans and the Swedes.

The only authority that sometimes could restore peace in these cities was that of the bishops, but even they were often unable to create goodwill between the richer and poorer classes.

The greatest disaster, however, happened to the South-western Provinces of Galicia and Volhynia. These fertile lands, the gateway into Europe, fell into the hands of their Western neighbours, and for many centuries to come the Orthodox population there had to endure subjugation to the unfriendly rule of the

Roman Catholics.   Yet, at first, that part of the country had been
the least affected by the Tartar invasion, and normal life in it had
been more quickly and fully restored.

Under the able leadership of Daniel, Prince of Galich (d. 1264),
the South-Western Provinces had become the centre of a Russian
revival, but the ambitious prince took a line opposite to that
pursued by his contemporary, Alexander Nevski, and this led
to his defeat.   Alexander accepted the Tartar yoke, but he
fought stubbornly against the Western aggressors, because he saw
that the threat to Russian integrity was greater from the Latin
world than from the Orient.   Daniel thought differently.   He
was determined to get rid at once of the Tartars, and as he could not
achieve this without foreign aid, he opened secret negotiations
with the Western Christians.   The Pope promised military help
on condition that Daniel should make his submission to Rome.
The Russian prince was, however, a staunch Orthodox Christian
and had no desire to leave his Church, yet under the pressure of
circumstances he played the rôle of a prospective convert.   As a
concession, he allowed the Latin emissaries to come to his country.
His policy of delay and compromise was a complete failure.   The
populace was openly hostile to Rome.   The Pope, seeing Daniel's
reluctance to fulfil his pledge, refrained from sending military help ;
but the Tartars got cognisance of Daniel's designs and, without
further delay, invaded Galicia and thoroughly devastated it.
Daniel died, a broken-hearted man.   It is true that he received
from the Pope a king's crown, but it was a poor substitute for his
grandiose scheme of liberating Russia from the Tartars with the
help of the Western Christians.   His policy had disastrous consequences.   He opened the gates to Western intervention, and
neither he nor his successors were able to close them again.

The Poles and the Hungarians started to attack Russian territory on the pretext that they were defending Papal rights,
violated by the Orthodox schismatics.   This policy was pursued
with particular vigour by King Kasimir of Poland (d. 1370),
who spent his long and successful reign in bitter struggle against
the Russians.   Encouraged by the Holy See, he treated his
campaigns for the conquest of Galicia as a holy crusade,
and he was joined by the neighbouring Hungarians.   In 1352,
he concluded an agreement with their King, Luis, which had
momentous consequences for the future of the lands now known
as the Ukraine.   According to this agreement, if Kasimir left

no male heir, all his Russian conquests were to go to the Hungarians; but, in return, they sold to him those Russian lands which they had been able to seize. At first, neither of the intruders made much progress, but in 1367 Kasimir occupied Galicia with its capital, Lvov, and added to it the Russian territories previously taken by Hungary and handed on to him by her King, Luis. His conquest was facilitated by the extinction of the House of Rurik in the South-Western Provinces. Its last representative, Prince Iuri II, died in 1323, and the party of boiars, or the landed nobility, keen to increase their privileges at the expense of the rest of the population, opposed the proposal to invite a member of another branch of the Rurik family to the throne. The Russian boiars, bearing in mind the fact that in Roman Catholic Poland and Hungary the aristocracy enjoyed far greater privileges than in Orthodox Russia, preferred to invite to the throne a foreign prince, hoping to satisfy in this way·their class interests. The peasants and middle classes opposed this policy and civil war flared up in the country. Galicia and Volhynia reached the depth of suffering and degradation in the fourteenth century. The Tartar hordes ravaged the unprotected country. Polish and Hungarian crusaders fought, sometimes against the Russians, and sometimes against each other. The Russian upper classes often behaved as traitors, and the loyal population which tried to defend the land laboured under the serious disadvantage of having no recognised leader. Yet, in spite of all these handicaps, it is doubtful whether the integrity of Russian territory would have been lost if another and unexpected Power had not appeared on the scene. It drove a deep wedge into Russian dominions, separated Galicia and Volhynia from the North-Eastern Provinces, and fatally undermined the strength of Russian resistance. This Power was Lithuania. Divided into many small tribes, the Lithuanians had lived from time immemorial in the marshy lands along the banks of the rivers Niemen and Vistula. Being neither Germanic nor Slavonic, they took little part in the history of Eastern Europe, and the Russians treated them as inoffensive barbarians. The collapse of Russia and the new pressure which the Teutonic Knights began to exert on the western frontier altered the situation. Under the leadership of Mindovg (d. 1263), who assumed the title of Grand Prince, the Lithuanians began to expand towards the east, chiefly along the valley of the Dnieper, where only a scattered Russian population

was left after the Tartar invasion. At first, this movement was
slow and cautious, but, seeing that the Russians had no power to
oppose them, the Lithuanians struck boldly south, and Prince
Gedemin (1316–41), in 1321, captured Kiev, the ancient capital
of Russia, after a short but sharp struggle.

The Lithuanians were still heathen at the time of their victory,
and they behaved very differently from the Poles and Hungarians
towards the conquered Russians. They treated the Orthodox
Church with respect, and many of them embraced Eastern
Christianity. Gedemin himself became a patron of learning; he
built schools and churches where Orthodoxy and the Russian
language were taught, and his capital, Vilna, with its many
Orthodox churches and monasteries, looked a typical Russian
city.

His successor, Olgerd (1341–77), went even farther than his
father. He joined the Orthodox Church, married a Russian
princess and identified himself with the interests of the Russian
people. He greatly extended his realm, defeated the Tartars
and the Poles several times, and, for a while, brought to a
standstill the advance of Western intruders. An increasing
number of Russians began to look upon the Lithuanian princes as
their legitimate rulers, hoping to recover under their leadership
the territories they had lost to Latin Christendom. There was a
time in Russian history when it seemed that Vilna would be the
capital of the reborn nation and that post-Tartar Russia would
be governed by a Lithuanian dynasty, and not by the house of
Rurik.

This expectation was not fulfilled, however. On the contrary,
after Olgerd's death, the Russians and the Lithuanians found
themselves split into two opposite camps, and their lack of agreement undermined the strength of the Lithuanian State. Instead
of remaining a great political Power, it became a minor partner
of Poland, subordinate in every respect to its Western neighbour.
The decline of Lithuania was as rapid as had been its rise to
importance. The event which provoked these changes was the
conversion of Olgerd's son, Yagailo, to Roman Catholicism, in
1386.

Another city was destined to become the capital of the resur-
rected nation. The process of recovery from moral and physical
prostration found its centre in a town called Moscow. In the
fatal years following Alexander's death there was only one bit of

Russian territory which stood outside the bitter conflicts and enjoyed peace and orderly government, and this was a domain ruled by Daniel (*d.* 1303), the youngest son of Alexander Nevski.

There are cities which, like people, are marked by destiny. Such a place is Moscow. Both the dark and the bright sides of Russia's life are revealed in her history. The bizarre colours of her red, blue and green cupolas, and the unusual contours of her buildings, reflect the sensuousness of the Orient and the serenity of the North, two elements present in the mentality of her inhabitants. Cruelty and mercy, oppression and tolerance, holiness and lust made in turn a strong appeal both to the rulers and to the people of Moscow. Her Kremlin and her streets are associated with the most heroic and the most shameful deeds of her national history. All that Russia possesses, good and bad, finds its expression in the life of that city, which appeared on the scene of Russian history in its gloomiest hour, and which has since governed the fortunes of her people.

Little is known about the origin of Moscow. The name is mentioned for the first time in the Chronicle of the year 1147. During the Tartar invasion, Moscow was destroyed, but it was soon rebuilt, and allotted to Daniel at the time of his father's death, when he was still a child (1263). During the twenty-seven years of his rule, he transformed the insignificant little town into an important centre of national revival. He achieved this by refusing to take part in the quarrels which absorbed the energy of his brothers and relatives, and by concentrating on the improvement of his small principality.

Daniel was a deeply religious man; he had no taste for war, no ambition to acquire the title of Grand Prince; he was a wise and thrifty landlord, and his position within his domain was different from that of other princes. Most of them had to share their power with the boiars and City Councils; they were still keen to exchange smaller towns for larger, and they were far from being the indisputable rulers of the territory under their control. Daniel, on the contrary, was a true master in his small borough. Moscow had neither a local aristocracy nor wealthy and influential merchants who claimed to share the power of the ruler. The security of his dominions attracted an ever-increasing number of refugees from other parts of the country. These newcomers received from Daniel permission to settle on his land, and they treated the prince as the sole master of the whole region. So

Moscow inaugurated a new form of paternal monarchy, which provided the needed cure for a nation rent asunder by the rivalry of the princes and the incursion of foreign invaders.

Daniel considerably increased his possessions by the purchase of neighbouring lands, for he had money, which other princes, who fought each other, always lacked. His policy of peaceful extension was continued by his second son, Ivan, surnamed "Kalita", or "the money bag" (d. 1341). Under him, Moscow became the seat of the Metropolitans of all Russia and thus secured the spiritual ascendancy over all other cities in the country. Ivan, like his father, had no interest in military matters; he was a good administrator and, above all, an excellent financier. He differed radically from other princes in his attitude to the Tartars. Instead of opposing the Mongols, he entered into collaboration with them and offered to be responsible for the collection of taxes due from Russia to the Khans. He was so efficient in this that he gained the lasting favour of the Tartars. His success was of the greatest advantage to the Russians, for they were at last saved from the major horror of the Tartar yoke : the regular visits of rapacious and cruel tax collectors who were ready to plunder and massacre the people at the slightest provocation. For the first time after many years of war and destruction, the country began to recover.

The Principality of Moscow, because it enjoyed friendship with the Tartars, increased rapidly in strength and size, but Ivan did not once take up arms in order to acquire new lands. Money and diplomacy, not warfare, were his weapons. The overlord of Russia, Uzbek (1313–41), who was the first Khan convert to Mahometanism, was a much-dreaded ruler. He learned by experience, however, that his revenues from Russia had been steadily rising since Ivan had become responsible for order in the country, and so, instead of plundering the subjected people, as his predecessors had done, Uzbek restrained his hordes from further attacks and granted to Ivan the title of Grand Prince (1328). Ivan accepted it but did not exchange his beloved Moscow, where he was sole master, for the turbulent capital of Vladimir. He began to call himself Grand Prince of Moscow and of all Russia, and in this he was justified, for he was genuinely concerned with the welfare of the whole land. Whenever the integrity of Russia was threatened from outside, he defended it. He even persuaded the Tartars to oppose the Lithuanians and the Germans, who were trying to increase the territory under their control at the expense of Russia. Thus, from being the poor and despised slave of the Mongols, Ivan rose to the status of an ally, whose words commanded respect and under whose orders the fierce Tartars were ready to fight against Russia's enemies.

Ivan's success was due, however, not only to his sagacity. He advanced so rapidly to the position of leader of the nation because he had the backing of the Russian Church. At its head stood a man of outstanding ability and devotion, named Peter (*d.* 1326). Though a native of Volhynia, he gave all his moral support to Ivan, for he realised that in Moscow, and not in his native Volhynia, was the true centre of the country's liberation. Peter himself had no fixed abode; he, like his predecessors, Cyril (*d.* 1281) and Maxim (*d.* 1305), travelled from one city to another, maintaining in this way the spirit of national unity in a land split into many rival principalities. His favourite town, however, was Moscow, and his visits there became more and more frequent. Ivan was a great church-builder. He erected in Moscow its first cathedral, dedicated to the Archangel Michael, which afterwards became the burial-place of all Grand Princes and Tsars. At the express desire of Peter, Ivan also built another cathedral (in Russia several cathedrals are often found in the same city), dedicated to the Assumption, and Peter ordered his body to be buried there. This was an event of great importance. The presence in Moscow of the tomb of one so highly revered, by all the people, elevated the city to a place of pre-eminence and helped Peter's successor, Theognost (*d.* 1352), to overcome the opposition of other princes and to make Moscow his permanent residence. Thus, during Ivan's reign, the political and ecclesiastical supremacy of Moscow was firmly established. The walls and the cathedrals of the Kremlin [1] built by him became the sacred scroll on which the history of the nation was to be inscribed by all succeeding generations.

The work of national restoration, so well started by Daniel, Ivan and the Metropolitan Peter, was brought to the verge of collapse in 1352, when the Black Death from India swept across the whole country, carrying away the greater proportion of the population. Ivan's able son, Simeon the Proud (1341–53), together with his sons and brothers, perished during the epidemic.

[1] The Kremlin is the inner fortified part of Moscow.

The country was depopulated and weakened, and Ivan the Fair, Simeon's successor, was not able to cope with the new problems. Moscow was in danger of losing her pre-eminence. The situation was again saved by a leader of the Church—this time by Alexis, Metropolitan of Moscow (1353–78). He was the first representative of the Russian hierarchy to take an active part in the government of the country. Himself a native of Moscow, he was a scholar and a statesman; he knew Greek (a rare accomplishment in that century among the Russians) and was a man of wide interests and knowledge. During the short reign of Ivan the Fair (1352–59), and during the infancy of his son and heir, Dmitri (d. 1389), Alexis acted as regent. His tact, ability and unselfish devotion to the welfare of the country overcame all obstacles and helped Moscow to maintain her ascendency. Alexis' policy was that of Alexander Nevski—submission to the East, and stubborn resistance to the West.

He was especially successful in securing the favour of the Mongols, and, here, his being a dignitary of the Church was a great asset to him. The traditional respect which the Tartars showed to the clergy was increased in his case by a cure which he performed on Taidula, the mother of Khan Khanibek (1342–57). This influential and domineering lady became the devoted friend of her healer. Her friendship proved of special value after the murder of her husband by his son Berdibek (1357–59). The new Khan was a cruel despot, but the genuine awe with which he regarded his mother enabled her to protect her favourite bishop. Alexis' main concern was the rapid growth of the Lithuanian Principality. Its Grand Prince, Olgred (1339–77), aimed at the incorporation of the whole of North-East Russia. The South-West Provinces were in his hands already. The new enemy was bold enough to attack even Moscow, and its suburbs were burnt down by the Lithuanian army in 1367. This new danger coming from the West made even more imperative the political unification of Russia, for the Lithuanian advance was made possible chiefly by the rivalries amongst the Russians themselves.

The city republics of Novgorod and Pskov and the principalities of Tver and Riazan were the main political rivals of Moscow, for the other cities and principalities were by now too small, and too dependent on Moscow, to cause much trouble. The Metropolitan Alexis was not afraid to use both his political and his ecclesiastical powers to reduce the remaining outposts of provincial exclusiveness to submission. He was especially resolute in dealing with Tver, where a local feud opened the doors to Lithuanian intervention. He even temporarily excommunicated the princes of Tver and of Smolensk because they were plotting with the Lithuanians. He imposed a similar punishment upon the Prince of Susdal, who started a war against his brother. This imposition of ecclesiastical punishment for causing political disturbances was a novelty in Russia, but it was approved by the best men of the nation, such as St. Sergius of Radonezh, because the very survival of Christianity in Russia depended on the political consolidation of the country.

The policy of Alexander Nevski, steadily followed by the Princes of Moscow, achieved through the work of Alexis the long-awaited victory. Three years after his death, the army of reunited Russia was able for the first time to strike a fatal blow against the Tartars. The victory of Kulikovo Pole (1380) was prepared by St. Alexis and inspired by his friend and disciple, St. Sergius of Radonezh.

CHAPTER V

ST. SERGIUS OF RADONEZH

ST. SERGIUS, Abbot of Radonezh (*d.* 1392), was one of the most remarkable men Russia has ever produced. He is a landmark in the history of his nation, and no one illustrates better than he the new religious outlook which made possible the cultural growth and expansion of the Russian nation. He is one of those exceptional leaders whose influence never ceases to make itself felt, and whose popularity remains unshaken throughout the whole course of history. His message makes the same appeal to Russian Christians of the twentieth century as it did to the Christians of his own time.[1]

St Sergius was born in the city of Rostov, probably in 1314. His parents were victims of the civil wars and had to flee from their native town. They found refuge in a small village called Radonezh, some fifty miles north of Moscow. There they lived as ordinary Russian peasants, and St. Sergius can therefore be truly called the peasant saint of Russia, the man who knew all the sorrows and joys of the peasant's lot, and who was familiar with all peasant crafts. He was a slow boy who mastered with difficulty the rudiments of education available in the Russia of his time. He could just read and write, and his only sources of instruction were the Slavonic Bible and the Services of the Orthodox Church. But, limited as these were, they represented some of the greatest treasures known to mankind: the religious ardour of the Hebrew Psalter and of the Old Testament Prophets; the theological inspiration of Christian hymns and prayers; the splendour of the Byzantine ritual and the uniqueness of the Gospels—all these were known to him from his early days. At the age of twenty, Bartholomew (this was the name of St. Sergius before he took monastic vows), in company with his elder brother Stephen, went into the wild forest which surrounded their village. The brothers built a timber hut and a tiny chapel, which they dedicated to the Life-giving Holy Trinity. There they intended to spend the rest of their lives in prayer and meditation. Stephen,

[1] The full story of his life is given in *St. Sergius, Builder of Russia*, by N. Zernov, S.P.C.K., 1939.

however, was not able to stand the hardships of life in the Russian wilderness. The danger from wild beasts, the scarcity of food, and, above all, the cold of the Russian winter drove him back to the town. There he entered one of the regular monasteries, but Bartholomew remained in the forest. For several years he lived quite alone, unknown to anybody. These years of untold trials and privations were the final tests of his character. He was victorious: he mastered his mind and body, disciplined his entire being and thus made himself ready for the service of God and of his people.

Eventually, he was discovered by some peasants, and soon people began to come in increasing numbers to ask the advice of this unusual anchorite. Some decided to join him. St. Sergius never invited anybody, but neither did he ever refuse anyone. Gradually a community grew round him, and he was elected as its Abbot. The sense of peace which emanated from him, his loving kindness and, above all, his complete confidence in God, which made him singularly free from any fear and hesitation, were the sources of his influence and attraction.

The Metropolitan Alexis of Moscow was one of those who were deeply impressed by him. Several times, St. Sergius went at his request to see the princes who endangered the national effort towards unity and freedom by their quarrels. Alexis wanted to appoint the humble monk as his successor, but St. Sergius firmly refused this honour. He was not called to govern but to serve, and he never used any authority except moral persuasion. He possessed, however, the singular gift of changing the hearts even of the hardest and least morally sensitive of men.

On his errands St. Sergius had to meet princes guilty of perjury and other crimes, but his voice of Christian admonition made even them ready to amend their evil ways. His reputation spread far and wide and he became a recognised spiritual leader of the nation, so that it was to him that the Grand Prince Dmitri turned for advice in the critical hour of Russia's struggle for liberation.

The wise and firm rule of Alexis, which preserved the unity of the country during Dmitri's infancy, made the young Prince powerful as no other ruler of Russia had been since the time of the Tartar invasion. The Russians had by now so recovered their sense of independence that Dmitri decided to erect round his capital the stone walls which were forbidden by the Tartars. This act provoked the suspicion of the Mongols, and their Khan,

Mamai, decided to inflict an exemplary punishment upon the dis-
obedient Russians. An army 400,000 strong was gathered against
Moscow. As in the thirteenth century, the attack on Russia
from the East was supported by the Christian West. Yagailo,
Prince of Lithuania, promised to assist the Tartars; the Republic
of Genoa provided the Mongols with military experts and modern
armaments. Russia stood alone against her formidable enemy.

Dmitri of Moscow cannot be called a great ruler, but at that
critical moment in his nation's history he proved a worthy leader.
He realised that what was at stake was not his personal fame or
courage, but the very existence of the Russians as a Christian
people. There was a real greatness about his conduct during those
decisive months. He made all the necessary military preparations
and concluded an alliance with the rest of the Russian princes,
persuading them to forget their petty rivalries and old feuds.
Then, when he had to come to the final decision, he went to seek
the sanction of a man whose moral judgment and wisdom could
be trusted by the country. Prince Dmitri chose to consult St.
Sergius, who, now that Alexis was dead, was the living representative of the conscience of the whole nation.

On an early autumn day, August 18th, 1380, Dmitri, accompanied by his closest friends, paid a visit to the saint. The
Tartars had already crossed the borders, and the Russian army
was gathered south of Moscow, in Kolomna, ready to start on its
march. No Russian heart can remain unmoved at the mention
of this solemn hour in Russian history. There was a striking
contrast between the strong, armed men, the best warriors of
the country, full of anxiety and concern, and the old monk,
serene and peaceful, standing in the midst of his disciples.
Prince Dmitri was afraid to take the last step on his own responsibility; there was still a possibility of laying down arms,
of imploring mercy in the hope of appeasing the wrath of the
Tartars. It was a moment of extreme tension; every one knew
the price which would have to be paid for a wrong decision.
Since the conversion of the Tartars to Mahometanism at the
beginning of the fourteenth century, their benevolent attitude to
the Church had changed to a hostile one. Russia's defeat would
therefore mean the massacre of the population, the profanation
of the churches, the suppression of Christianity. On the other
hand, submission would mean, probably, the destruction of the
leaders and the moral collapse of the people. Submission was

therefore more than dangerous, but was there any chance of successful resistance? Were not the Tartars always victorious? Had they not suppressed all Russian attempts at liberation during the last century and a half? Such were the questions in every mind, and the eyes of all were fixed upon the old monk.

St. Sergius, usually so reticent, was this time firm and explicit. Confronted with supreme danger, he did not evade its challenge. He gave his blessing to Dmitri and, promising him victory, urged the Prince to meet the attack of the enemy in the open steppes of the south. His last words were, " Go forward and fear not. God will help thee." On August 20th the Russians started towards the south. It was an army which included men from the four corners of the land. Never before had the country seen the Princes of Moscow, of Vladimir, of Serpukhov, of Rostov, of Pskov, of Murom, of Suzdal, marching in a body. The army advanced rapidly. On August 26th it crossed the river Oka; on September 6th it reached the river Don. The Russians were once more in the open steppes where their forefathers had been overwhelmed by the irresistible waves of Mongolian invaders. The military council was assembled and the question debated whether the army ought to cross the river. Cautious voices were raised in favour of waiting, but Dmitri gave the order to proceed further into the unknown plains of the south. He was at that moment the true leader of young Russia. He wanted to meet her enemy in the heart of the steppes, in the stronghold of those who for so long had kept his country in fear and submission. The determination displayed by Prince Dmitri was due to St. Sergius' influence. The old monk stood behind the military leader of the Russian nation. On this fateful day of final decision, a special envoy, sent from Radonezh, reached the camp. He brought from St. Sergius a message addressed to Dmitri and through him to the rest of the Russian men. Its content was as follows: " Be in no doubt, my lord; go forward with faith and confront the enemy's ferocity; and fear not, for God will be on your side."

On September 8th, 1380, the two armies met at last. No battle in Russian history can be compared with that of Kulikovo Pole. Here occurred the clash between two irreconcilable powers. Four hundred thousand nomads, with their camels and horses and inspired by the sight of the Crescent, faced a much smaller army of Russians, gathered under the eight-pointed Eastern Cross. Kulikovo Pole occupies a place in history similar to that of the

battle of Poitiers (732), when France saved the West from
Mahometan invasion; or to the fatal defeat of Kosovo in 1389,
which marked the beginning of the five-centuries-long Moslem
domination over the Christians of the Balkans.

The struggle was fierce and the losses on both sides were
enormous. At first the Tartars had the upper hand but, at the
critical moment, when the main Russian force was precipitated
into a disorderly retreat, the fortunes of war were suddenly
reversed by an unexpected attack of Russian reserves, and a
crushing blow was inflicted upon the Mongols. St. Sergius'
prophecy was fulfilled: the advance of the Mahometans was
arrested; Russia was to remain a Christian country.

The victory of Kulikovo Pole was not, however, the end of the
Tartar domination. Khan Tokhtamysh (1380–95), who murdered his unfortunate predecessor, Mamai, made an unexpected
attack on Russia. He failed at first to capture Moscow but,
discovering that Prince Dmitri was not in the city, he offered a
truce to its inhabitants which, once accepted, he immediately
violated, and massacred the entire population. The annihilation
of the Capital induced Dmitri to recognise once more the
sovereignty of the Tartar Khans, but the relations between them
and the Russians were altered. The Russians no longer looked
on the Tartars as invincible; the latter were no longer sure of
always having the upper hand. From the end of the fourteenth
century, the Tartar yoke meant little more than the payment of
tribute, and the two nations began to treat each other as equals
rather than as conqueror and conquered.

St. Sergius performed a miracle with the Russians: he
changed a defeated people into the builders of a great Empire.
He did not, however, employ any of the methods which are usually
associated with the work of great leaders and reformers. He never
preached a single sermon; he did not write a single book; all his
life he behaved like the humblest, the least distinguished of men—
and yet it was he who was selected by the unanimous voice of the
nation as its teacher and liberator. The secret of St. Sergius'
influence lies in the singular integrity of his life : his sole activity
was in the service of the Holy Trinity, and he became in himself
such a faithful reflection of divine harmony and love that all who
came in contact with him grew aware of the Heavenly Vision.
The Christian faith that God is the Holy Trinity implies that the
Creator of this world is the perfect community of Three Persons

whose relation is that of mutual love. St. Sergius was not a theologian in the accepted sense of the word. He never wrote or spoke about the Trinitarian doctrine, but he was himself a living example of that divine Unity in Freedom which is the essence of the Christian revelation of the nature of God. His biography contains the following passage: " St. Sergius built the Church of the Holy Trinity as a mirror for his community, that through gazing at the divine Unity they might overcome the hateful divisions of this world."

This short statement summarises the life work of St. Sergius and his contribution to the spiritual growth of the Russian nation. Its most remarkable feature was a clear realisation of the supreme importance of the Trinitarian teaching for the moral rebirth of a nation. The change which took place in Russia in the time of St. Sergius was profound and far-reaching. The nation was delivered from a paralysing fear and it recovered its sense of strength. He not only helped the Russians to embrace the inspiring ideal of a Christian society based on unity in freedom, but he also convinced them that there was a road leading to its practical application. The vision of a country living as a united family, and observing the precepts of the Church, became a driving force behind the people's actions. The miraculous victory over the superior forces of the Tartars so stirred the imagination of the Russians that a new sense of messianic vocation flared up in their midst. The first part of the fifteenth century was therefore a period when the new Russia of Moscow was spiritually born, when the foundations on which the Moscow Tsardom was erected, in the course of the next two centuries, were laid. St. Sergius cannot, however, be called the architect of that order, for his teaching was much broader than those ideas which were realised under the rule of the Moscow autocrats.

St. Sergius is a prophetic figure. He is the link between two distinct Russias: the one which became a great political power joining Asia and Europe, and the other Russia of a free Christian community, the Russia of saints, philosophers and artists which has remained, in spite of many disappointments and failures, the aspiration of her people in every age.

CHAPTER VI

THE MOSCOW TSARDOM AND THE RUSSIAN CHURCH

St. Sergius freed the Russians from the spell of fear and defeatism which had kept them in chains for more than a hundred and fifty years. The strong current of new life flowing from him transformed the disheartened people into men of courage and vision.

On the Russian plain a mighty Empire was born which incorporated many lands and races. Rarely has its eastward expansion been the result of conquest; usually it has been the fruit of gradual and peaceful colonisation. Its pioneers were neither daring military adventurers nor enterprising merchants. They were hard-working peasants and humble monks—the disciples of St. Sergius. These monks, inflamed by the spirit of faith and resolution which they had caught from their teacher, left the narrow stretches of cultivated land along the river valleys to which hitherto the bulk of the Russian population had confined itself. They fearlessly penetrated into the depths of unexplored forests and marshes and there founded their settlements. They were no longer afraid, as their fathers had been, to leave human habitations behind; neither cold, nor hunger, nor wild beasts, nor hostile tribes could hinder them. The monks, who followed the rule of community life, of manual labour and of open hospitality, introduced by St. Sergius, spread the light of Christianity all over the vast plain, and their message reached even the most remote regions of the extreme north, for many of them were also outstanding missionaries.

Over fifty new monasteries were founded by the disciples of St. Sergius during his lifetime; fifty others were started by the men of the next generation. St. Abraham of Galich, St. Methodius of Peshnosh, St. Paul and St. Sylvester of Obnorsk, St. Athanasius, the Iron Staff, St. Savva of Storozhev, St. Cyril and St. Therapont of the White Lake—these are some of the best-known names among these pioneers. They had no desire to enlarge the frontiers of the Russian State; they went out in search of places for undisturbed prayer and quiet labour; but, once they had settled down, other Russians followed in their steps. First came

42

those who wanted to join their religious communities; later, devout peasants, accompanied by their families, built their settlements near the cells of the monks. The peasants discovered a new freedom in the inaccessible forests; they were better protected there from the Tartars and were more independent of their own officials. The monks, seeing themselves surrounded by peasants' huts, pushed still farther, but the peasants, having once uprooted themselves, found it easy to move again. They followed the monks, and thus a spontaneous movement of colonisation started, which carried with it an ever-increasing number of people.

Such a flow of population could not escape the notice of the princes, and they began to claim the territories inhabited by their former taxpayers. As a result a new and stronger State came into being, but its builders had to face three formidable tasks. The first one was the liberation of the country from the Mongols; the second was the reopening of communications with the rest of Christendom, through the recovery of the sea coast seized by the Western neighbours during the Tartar invasion; and the third was the establishment of a new political order which could protect the independence of the Russian people.

None of these was an easy proposition, and the Russians had to start their work under adverse conditions. The long subjugation to the Mongols had retarded the normal growth of the nation; the population was scattered, driven from the fertile plains of the south into the cold and inhospitable marshy lands of the north; and the Russians were, besides, deprived of stimulating contact with the more advanced countries of the West, and forced to rely upon their own limited resources. The road to unity and freedom was steep and narrow, but the Russians were not dismayed by these obstacles. Their chief difficulty was that they had to deal with all their problems simultaneously. As soon as they made progress in the east, they were threatened in the west; if they advanced towards the Baltic Sea, they were immediately attacked in the steppes of the south; and they could deal successfully with their hostile neighbours only if they were ready to endure the autocratic rule of their Tsars.

Living in a land utterly devoid of natural lines of protection, with a population inadequate in numbers, with a soil yielding less than that of neighbouring countries and requiring more labour, each individual Russian was asked to make infinitely greater sacrifices for his country, and to bear in its defence hardships and privations severer than any suffered by members of other nations.

From the fourteenth century till the present day, the Russians have had to accept a state of perpetual mobilisation as the only alternative to the collapse of their entire defensive system. Many of the negative features of the Russian political order, like the extensive powers given to the Tsars, the serfdom of the peasants and the inadequate safeguards of personal liberty, arose out of the extremely unfavourable circumstances in which the nation had to labour for the recovery and preservation of its independence. The Russians of Moscow were obliged to give up their individual freedom, which their ancestors cherished so highly, not because they had ceased to value it, but because they realised they could protect their land only if they were ready to establish a monarchy built on the same pattern as the Empire of the Mongols. But the spirit behind it was different. Its inspiration came from the Christian Church, with its belief in freedom and in the value of each person. Though the political and economic system was often oppressive, yet people were inwardly free, for they knew that they were all brothers, equal members of the redeemed community.

There is no better illustration of the curious mixture of Christian fellowship with Oriental despotism than the story of serfdom in Russia—the greatest blunder in its history. Serfdom resulted from confused political thinking; it arose from the attempt to secure economic stability and better defences by binding the peasants to the soil. Everyone in Russia had to serve the community: the landed gentry formed a permanent militia, so the peasants in return had to provide their defenders with free labour. All Russians were not ready to carry this heavy burden. The open steppes of the south and the forests of the north offered freedom to those who were not afraid of risk and adventure. The flight of these Russians made the lot of those who remained behind still harder, and in order to stop this flow of population the Government gave to the gentry an increasing power of control over the peasants, until, in the eighteenth century, they became the private property of the landowners.

Nothing is more foreign to the Russian mind than an idea of inherited inequality among men. Serfdom, therefore, was, from start to finish, an abuse, never a law.

The peasants could never be reconciled to the loss of their

freedom, and, even in serfdom, they stubbornly retained their community organisation, with their elected elders and their primitive village parliament (mir). In spite of oppression, they preserved the sense of equality and human dignity, and in this they were greatly assisted by the Church, which reminded all its members of this truth by communicating both the serfs and their masters from the same chalice, and by insisting that they all had to ask pardon of each other before partaking of the divine Eucharist.

The powerful uprisings of the rural population which several times shook the very foundation of the Russian State (the revolts of Bolotnikov, 1606–7, of Stenka Razin, 1670–71, of Bulavin, 1707, and of Emelian Pugachev, 1773–75), bear witness to the undying thirst for freedom fostered in the Russian heart by the teaching and practice of the Orthodox Church. These rebellions were part of a heavy price the country had to pay for the mistakes committed by its rulers, most of which arose from the exceptional difficulties under which the Russians had to strive as the result of the disaster of the Tartar invasion.

After many efforts and disappointments, the Russians at last created a strong centralised authority, such as the defence of the country required. It was achieved under the leadership of the Grand Princes of Moscow, who became at the end of the fifteenth century the Tsars of all Russia. Their rise to power was a gradual process; the rulers of Moscow, Basil I (1389–1425), Basil II (1425–62), Ivan III (1462–1505), Basil III (1505–33), moved step by step with great caution. They all had much in common: their cast of mind, their policy and their gifts and limitations conformed to the same pattern. None of them was an outstanding person, but each of them was instinctively a ruler. They advanced slowly but always in the right direction, and therefore performed an indispensable service to the nation, helping it to rise from its bed of sickness and prostration.

The Princes of Moscow were thrifty landlords, who regarded the growth of their Principality in terms of the increase of their personal property. In their wills they distributed not only their gold, silver and furs among their children, but also the towns and the provinces of their realm, which they treated as mere private possessions, acquired, as they were, chiefly by purchase and negotiation. They had nothing of the spirit of bravery and military adventure so prominently displayed by other members of the

House of Rurik.   They possessed, also, little sense of honour.   As
long as the Tartars were strong, they served them more obediently
than any other Russian prince, but, as soon as they had gathered
enough strength to oppose the Khans, they boldly proclaimed
themselves the successors of the Byzantine Emperors.   They were
devoutly Orthodox and accepted without question the authority
of the Church.   They shared with the rest of the nation the conviction of the sacred mission assigned to Russia by God, and they
never failed to use every opportunity for the advancement of the
great cause.

The first visible fruits of their patient labours were reaped
during the reign of Ivan III, surnamed the Great (1462–1505).
Under him, Russia made a striking advance in dealing with her
three great problems.   The autocracy of the Moscow Tsars was
established; the eastward drive of Lithuania was stopped, and
part of the lost Russian territory was recovered; finally, the
Tartar yoke was repudiated and Ivan assumed the title of Tsar.
The final liberation of the country from submission to the Mongols
was achieved without bloodshed, the balance of power being so
obviously in favour of Moscow that the Tartars were unable to
oppose the Russians.[1]

The end of the Tartar domination coincided with the absorption by Moscow of the remaining principalities.   None of them
was able to offer much resistance except the wealthy city of
Novgorod.   It was the last outpost into the Western world left to
the Russian people, and a lively trade was carried on by its enterprising and freedom-loving citizens.   Moscow and Novgorod had
little sympathy with each other.   Novgorod stood for individual
responsibility; its people mixed freely with foreigners, and the
unruly population was ready to defend its traditional liberties
against all those who had any designs upon them.   Moscow stood
for obedience and caution, was suspicious of all strangers and was
prepared to sacrifice freedom for the sake of unity and power.

Moscow and Novgorod needed each other, and the success
of their common struggle against both Eastern and Western

---

[1] The rejection of the yoke did not mean, however, that the danger from
the Mongols was at an end.   Till the incorporation of the Crimea in 1783,
the Russians continued to suffer from the incursions of the nomads, and the
southern steppes remained half-deserted, because they were exposed to the
Tartars' sudden attack which brought death or slavery to all who happened to
be in their way.

aggressors depended on their collaboration. But from the middle of the fifteenth century their relations had been strained, each side considering that the other did not keep to the terms of their alliance. Moscow accused Novgorod of secret negotiations with Lithuania; Novgorod retorted that Moscow interfered unlawfully in the domestic affairs of the Republic.

In 1471, an open clash occurred. The citizens of Novgorod, expecting support from Lithuania, rejected Moscow's terms (which stipulated the rupture of all relations with their Western neighbours). Ivan III sent a strong army, and Novgorod was obliged to surrender. The Tsar showed at first great moderation and allowed Novgorod to retain its republican government. But when two further rebellions broke out and he had again to send his armies to storm the city, in 1478 and then in 1479, he lost patience and imposed severe terms upon the thrice-defeated citizens. The leading families were deported and scattered all over Russia. Self-government and the ancient liberties of the city were abolished. The unity of the central and northern provinces was thus achieved, but in a way which proved unfavourable to the nation. The door into Europe was shut, foreign trade came to a standstill, and the spirit of freedom and enterprise so prominently displayed by the people of Novgorod was extinguished.

The Grand Princes of Moscow at last became sole rulers of a vast country, and the problem arose of defining their place in the life of the nation. The answer to it was found in the belief that Moscow was the successor to Constantinople, and that her Tsars were the legitimate heirs of the Byzantine Emperors. The expansion of every nation, the growth of every empire is usually the outward sign of an inward conviction of the people that they have a special mission to perform. The striking transformation of the small Moscow principality into one of the largest States of the world was the result of the deep-rooted belief of her people that they were called to defend Eastern Orthodoxy, left without protection since the fall of Constantinople in 1453. The period of a hundred years between the battle of Kulikovo Pole in 1380 and the repudiation of the Tartar yoke in 1480 was the turning point in the destiny of the nation. Several important events, following each other in ever quicker succession, produced a deep impression upon the Russians. In 1380, they gained their first victory over the Mongols; in 1439, they heard, to their dismay, that the Byzantine Emperor and the Patriarch of Constantinople, those pillars of Eastern Orthodoxy, had surrendered their Church to the Latin heretics at the Council of Florence. Swift retribution followed, and Constantinople, the capital of Eastern Christendom, was taken away from the Greeks in 1453. In 1472, Ivan III married Sophia Paleologos, the niece of the last Emperor, and took as his coat-of-arms the two-headed Byzantine Eagle. In 1480, Ivan repudiated the Tartar yoke and proclaimed himself Tsar, or autocrat—a ruler independent of any other sovereign.

The Russians, together with the rest of the Eastern Christians, believed that the Church and the Empire were both instituted by God and were indispensible for the maintenance of true religion. The fall of Constantinople was, therefore, a shattering blow for them, and a feeling of doom spread all over the Christian East. But this did not last long, for the hope grew that Russia was chosen by God to resume the same work which was brought to a standstill by the apostasy of the Emperor and the sacking of the Great City.

Such was the origin of the belief in Moscow as the third and last Rome, a belief which had far-reaching consequences for the history of the nation, and which influenced profoundly the outlook of its people. Its universal acceptance was due to its Biblical roots. The Eastern Christians based their vision of a succession of kingdoms raised to pre-eminence by divine providence on the Book of the Prophet Daniel (II, 27–49, VII, 1–28, IX, 24–27). The prophecy of the Four Empires was interpreted in the light of the commentaries of St. Hippolytus (d. 223) who identified them with Babylon, Persia, the Empire of Alexander the Great, and Rome. During the ascendency of the Fourth Realm, the greatest events in human history were expected to take place, including the Second as well as the First Coming of the Messiah. The collapse of the western part of the Roman Empire in the fifth century did not affect this conviction, for the Eastern Christians believed that Constantinople was the New or Second Rome. They ascribed to her the same promises of indestructibility which were originally made in regard to Rome herself. When Moscow became the only capital among the Eastern Christians free from the control of the infidels, it was natural that she should be elevated to the position of the Third and Last Rome. Thus Moscow found herself linked with the ancient realms of the East, but her future, though bright with the aura of divine election, was, nevertheless, clouded by the sobering thought of impending punishment, if she proved unfaithful in the fulfilment of her great mission.

In these decisive years of the second part of the fifteenth century, when modern Europe was about to be born, the Russian people experienced a genuine sense of resurrection. After a long period of suffering, humiliation and despair, they were suddenly raised to a new life of freedom, power and glory. They felt themselves brought out of darkness into light and entrusted with the awe-inspiring task of being the guardians of true faith and worship for the rest of mankind. Philotheus, one of the Russian scholars, an elder of a monastery in Pskov, formulated this wide-spread belief in his epistle addressed to Basil III. He wrote: " The Church of old Rome fell for its heresy; the gates of the second Rome, Constantinople, were hewn down by the axes of the infidel Turks; but the Church of Moscow, the Church of the new Rome, shines brighter than the sun in the whole universe. Thou art the one universal sovereign of all Christian folk, thou shouldst hold the reins in awe of God; fear Him Who hath committed them to thee. Two Romes are fallen, but the third stands fast; a fourth there cannot be. Thy Christian kingdom shall not be given to another."

The claims of a country like Russia, lost in the dark forests of the far-off North, whose very existence was hardly realised in the Europe of the fifteenth century, to be the heir of the great Roman Empire, were not so ambitious and naïve as may appear. They were truly prophetic. Twenty-five years after Philotheus wrote his epistle, the Russian armies captured the Tartar fortresses of Kazan and Astrakhan, and the nation began to expand rapidly towards the east. A hundred years later the frontier of the country reached the Pacific Ocean, and in two hundred years' time the Northern Empire spread from the White Sea to the Black, and from the Baltic to Alaska.

The Russians took upon themselves the cultural mission of Byzantium; they became a link between East and West, the defenders and exponents of the order built on the foundation of Orthodox Christianity. The Russians could not, of course, reproduce that unique combination of the Christian, Hellenistic and Oriental elements of civilisation, which was the great achievement of the Byzantine Empire. They did not belong to the

Mediterranean commonwealth; they had never stood before the
majestic ruins of bygone empires; they had never read the annals
of their victories, crimes and achievements. The names of
Homer, Aristotle and Virgil conveyed nothing to them. They
were saved, therefore, from the danger of becoming mere imitators
of Byzantium, the temptation which crippled the development of
the southern Slavs. The latter were so fascinated by Constantinople that they exhausted themselves in vain attempts to copy
their august neighbour. The Russians followed their own path,
and they created a new order, quite distinct from that of the
Eastern Empire but inspired by the same ultimate vision of
life. Moscow was little indebted to Constantinople in politics,
economics and social organisation, but it was conspicuously the
heir of Byzantium in the realm of the spirit, in art, religion and,
especially, worship. Here, the Russians followed the true tradition
of the Second Rome, and were able to enrich it along their own
lines. It was through the wealth of the Byzantine liturgy that
they entered so fully into the cultural inheritance of the ancient
world.

Rome bequeathed to mankind the idea of law, discipline and
order, and these elements of her civilisation were later incorporated in the imposing system of the Roman Catholic Church.
Constantinople introduced into the life of Christendom the unique
intellectual and artistic achievements of Greece; and the gift of
the Second Rome was the formulation of Christian doctrine.
Moscow could not compete in either of these spheres with her
great predecessors. Her special domain was the art of Christian
living; the application of Christianity to the corporate daily life of
the people. And here her contribution was of the first importance.
Her ideal was that of a Christian State living as one family, in
which every man, from the Sovereign down to the poorest and
least educated of its members, could have his full share of spiritual
benefits and joys. The sense of being one community experienced
by the Russians was spontaneous and organic. It arose not from
obedience to authority, nor from the idea of duty, nor from
intellectual agreement: it was due to a pattern of life, a rhythm
of existence which was lovingly designed, built and followed by
the entire population. Innumerable Church customs and home
traditions provided the content of that ritual of daily life which
was the most distinctive mark of Russian culture. The Russian

interpretation of Christianity was more artistic than intellectual, being based on the vision of the Church as a living organism rather than an institution. Salvation was conceived not so much in terms of the forgiveness of the sins of the individual, as a part of a healing and sanctifying process which aimed at the transfiguration of men, of beasts and plants, and of the whole cosmos. St. Sergius was the first to give harmonious expression to this typically Russian approach to religion. He was able to fulfil the highest aspiration of the nation and he became the living example of unity in freedom (Sobornost). This achievement was, however, seldom within the reach of other Russians. Long centuries of mistakes, sufferings and trials separated them from their final goal—that of making their country a genuine family of Christian people. Even St. Sergius' disciples were not always able to follow in his path, and they split into opposite schools, each of which emphasised one side of their common inheritance. One of them, known under the nickname of " the Possessors ", laid stress on unity and greatly appreciated the beauty and dignity of ritual both in the conduct of worship and in daily life. The other, nicknamed " the Non-Possessors ", insisted on the importance of freedom and taught that nothing was more pleasing to God than a humble and contrite heart lovingly and freely obeying the Creator.

Several outstanding men in the sixteenth century represented those two parties. St. Joseph, the famous Abbot of Volotsk (1439–1515), Genadi, Archbishop of Novgorod (d. 1505), and Daniel, Metropolitan of Moscow (d. 1539), were the spokesmen of the Possessors. St. Nil of Sorsk (1433–1508), Prince Vassian Patrikeev (d. 1531) and St. Maxim the Greek (d. 1556) were the able exponents of the Non-Possessors' point of view. As long as both parties had their full share in the shaping of the country's destiny, Russian life was fresh and vigorous.

The Possessors greatly contributed to the artistic perfection of worship. They were also able administrators, and the monasteries built by them enjoyed order and prosperity. Their religious houses owned large estates, and, because they insisted that the monks were authorised to possess lands and to control the serfs who inhabited them, they received their nickname. The Possessors were the upholders of an autocracy and they were ready to allow the Sovereign to take a leading rôle in the government of the Church. They preached the doctrine that the Tsars ought to be loved and obeyed as fathers were obeyed by their children.

The Non-Possessors were scholars and mystics, men of learning and independent mind. Their most eloquent spokesman, St. Maxim the Greek, who was brought up in Italy, was one of the best-educated men of the century. They were not afraid to criticise, if necessary, the leaders of the State and of the Church. They insisted that monks ought to depend on their own labour and thus maintain their spiritual independence. They were also opposed to the persecution of heretics and taught that in a Christian State no one must be put to death for holding erroneous doctrines. In a century when, in the West, Roman Catholics and Protestants held, with equal vigour, that it was the duty of Christian Governors to execute heretics, the Russian Church alone contained an influential party which considered the practice as incompatible with the spirit of the Gospel.

Unfortunately, the co-existence of these two schools of thought was brought to an end by the intervention of the Tsar, Basil III. He had no children and decided, therefore, to divorce his wife and marry another woman. The Metropolitan, Varlaam (1511–21), who leaned towards the Non-Possessors, refused to sanction the Tsar's desire and was strongly supported by other leaders of his party. Such, however, was not the attitude of the Possessors. They declared that the future of the monarchy was of greater importance than the fate of a woman, and their spokesman, Daniel, expressed his willingness to re-marry the Sovereign. Basil gladly availed himself of this offer. The Tsar secured Daniel's election to the Metropolitan seat in 1522 and was remarried by him in the next year. The fruit of this wedlock was Ivan the Terrible (1533–84).

The opposition of the Non-Possessors had incurred the displeasure of the Tsar. The Possessors seized this opportunity to deal a blow at their opponents. St. Maxim and Prince Vassian were imprisoned, their supporters were scattered and the monasteries were closed. Russia in this suffered a heavy loss. At a time when the country had obtained independence and was about to embark on a great programme of reconstruction, the leadership in Church and State fell into the hands of a single party. It had some able men, but they did not represent the whole of Russia, and therefore they were responsible for the subsequent one-sided development of her political and cultural life.

The initial success of the Moscow Principality was the result of the close and friendly collaboration of its princes with the Church, but, when Basil, through his interference, upset the balance within the Christian community and violated its freedom, the relations between Church and State deteriorated and the nation was brought to the verge of collapse. This happened fifty years after the suppression of the Non-Possessors.

CHAPTER VII

IVAN THE TERRIBLE AND ST. PHILIP, METROPOLITAN OF MOSCOW

BASIL III died in 1533, leaving behind two small sons, the elder, Ivan, being only four years old. He and his brother had an unhappy childhood; they were neglected by their mother and ill-treated by the courtiers. They grew up embittered and revengeful. Ivan, highly strung and intelligent, was intensely religious, but he lacked balance—that quality which had made his ancestors so successful in achieving the unity of the nation. He was never sure of himself, always suspicious of others and, towards the end of his life, the helpless victim of his own cruelty and vice, which disintegrated his gifted personality.

Under him the Moscow Tsardom achieved great successes, but it also suffered some of its most serious reverses. Ivan was profoundly influenced by the teaching of the Possessors about the supreme power of the Tsars and firmly believed himself to be the divinely appointed head of the nation. He was the first autocrat on the throne of Moscow, and the Russians learned under him all the advantages and disadvantages of having a single ruler.

Ivan's reign falls into three periods. He started badly, but from 1547 he enjoyed, for thirteen years, one success after another and during this time the country reached the apex of its power and prosperity. From 1560 till the end of his reign (1584), he went back to his evil ways and plunged the nation into the turmoil of bitter social revolution.

Ivan was only thirteen years old when he ordered the arrest of a powerful but unpopular prince, Andrei Shuiski, and this was the beginning of his rule. As a boy he showed signs of insane cruelty towards both men and animals. Things moved from bad to worse, until a crisis occurred which for a time completely changed him. In 1547, a huge fire destroyed a large part of his capital. Many thousands of people were burnt alive, and the impressionable youth interpreted this calamity as divine punishment inflicted upon him. It was a moment in his life when he sincerely desired to amend his sinful life, and this opportunity

54

was seized by a remarkable priest, named Sylvester. Very little is known about his previous career except that he was a native of freedom-loving Novgorod. For twelve years (1547–59), he guided the Tsar and, as long as he was in control, the country flourished. Far-reaching reforms were introduced in the government; the army was reorganised and several campaigns were successfully fought.

Sylvester was a contributor to a book called *Domostroi* (the Home-builder). It contains a set of instructions, addressed to a youth, covering a large range of subjects, religious, moral and domestic. The philosophy of life expressed in it was typical of the mentality of those Russians who built up the new Empire of the North. The book enjoyed wide popularity and was read extensively till the time of Peter the Great's reforms. Its outlook was intensely ritualistic, but singularly free from clericalism. Though ascetic, it placed the Christian family above celibacy and monasticism; and, though severe in its treatment of men and fully recognising the power of sin in them, it was optimistic in its view of the ultimate destiny of mankind, for it trusted in the power of divine forgiveness and in the reality of regeneration. *Domostroi* advocated a code of behaviour which regulated the manner of speech, of gait and even of laughter, but it was not oppressive, for it sprang from a deep conviction of man's dignity and freedom. Sylvester described the purpose of human life as the glorification of the Creator. He was a great believer in the sacredness of each human being, and he was therefore resolutely opposed to serfdom. He wrote to his son: " I have not only liberated all my own serfs and endowed them, but I have also redeemed many serfs of other masters and given them their freedom. I have endeavoured to educate them, each according to his ability. Your mother did the same with the girls. At present many of my former serfs are priests, deacons or clerks, and each one does what he can in accordance with his natural disposition and the will of God."

Inspired by this idea, Sylvester introduced many reforms in the administration of the country, granting self-government to many provinces. The collection of taxes and the execution of justice were left in the hands of elected representatives. The Tsar under Sylvester's influence began the convocation of National Assemblies, which advised him on the conduct of foreign and home affairs. The following list illustrates the sequence of

important events which took place in Russia in those happy
years:—

1547. Ivan was crowned in Moscow as the first Russian Tsar,
heir and successor of the Byzantine Basileus. In the same
year technicians, printers and physicians were brought to
Russia from the West to teach arts and crafts and to start
new industries.

1547–1549. The solemn canonisation of forty-five Russian Saints
took place. They were chosen from different provinces of
the country, and this act strengthened the spiritual unity of
the nation, for most of these Saints had previously been
venerated only in their own districts.

1550. The National Assembly approved a new legal code.

1551. A Council of the Russian Church, known as that of the
Hundred Chapters, was held; many improvements were
introduced and the superiority of Russian Orthodoxy over
other branches of the Eastern Church was asserted.

1552. The Tartar Tsardom of Kazan was conquered.

1553. The first printing-press was set up in Moscow. Commercial relations with England were opened up via the
White Sea and Archangel.

1554–1555. The Tartar Tsardom of Astrakan was conquered.

1555. Khan Edigei, the ruler of Western Siberia, submitted to
the Tsar of Moscow. A large measure of local self-government was introduced.

1556. The military organisation of the country was greatly
improved.

1558. Russia began a successful campaign in the Baltic provinces
and her army reached the walls of Riga.

Even this brief summary of the achievements of the first years
of Ivan's reign shows the amount of intense activity that took
place in all spheres of national life. After a long period of prostration, Russia had awakened, and her people were determined
to make up for the time lost during the two centuries of their
subjugation to the Mongols.

At that time, the seat of the Metropolitan of Moscow was
occupied by Makari (1542–63). He shared the Possessors' outlook and did not take an active part in the reforms. Yet he
was not opposed to them and his reputation for learning and
piety stood high.

He spent many years in completing a monumental work in twelve volumes, entitled *Monthly Readings*. He collected in it all available religious literature, either translated or written in Russian, and subdivided it into portions suitable for daily reading. It contained commentaries on the Bible, lives of the Saints, the works of the Fathers, sermons, descriptions of journeys, and other edifying information. Makari worked for twenty years on this collection, and he inaugurated a literary movement of importance which spread all over the country.

The lives of the newly-canonised Saints were composed, the history and geography of Russia written, and all these books were adorned with large numbers of finely executed illustrations. *The History of the House of Rurik*, for instance, alone, had 16,000 miniatures.

The political revival of the country reached its most spectacular point when, in 1552, the Russians stormed Kazan, the formidable stronghold of the Tartars. Thousands of Russian captives were liberated by the victorious army, and for the first time the Mongols had to acknowledge the sovereignty of the Russian Tsar. Ivan behaved with magnanimity towards the defeated enemy. The conquered were allowed to retain all their possessions, their religious freedom was respected, and they became loyal subjects of Moscow. This conquest flung open the gates for the advance towards the East, and the Russian Empire began rapidly to spread over Siberia. These splendid achievements were commemorated in the Church of St. Basil, erected in the " Red Square " [1] in Moscow to record in architecture the significance of this victory. Built by two Russians, Borma and Postnik, it is the most original of all the churches in Moscow. Its domes are of different shapes and colours, representing the diverse cultures of Asia, and they express the conviction that Russia had a mission to bring the light of the Gospel to Asiatic peoples. St. Basil's reveals that unique fusion of Oriental and Christian elements which has become the distinctive feature of Russian culture.

In the midst of these successes another change occurred in the life of the Tsar, but this time it was a return to the depravity of his youth. Ivan became tired of his spiritual adviser and, encouraged by the courtiers who resented the high position occupied by a simple parish priest, he ordered Sylvester to

---

[1] The Russian word for " red " also means " fair " or " beautiful."

leave Moscow in 1559. In 1560, he lost his much-loved wife, Anastasia Romanova, and, no longer checked by her good influence, he plunged again into the dark passions and lusts of his early years. Ivan removed, one after another, by execution or exile, his gifted civil and military collaborators and surrounded himself with a crowd of base and unscrupulous men who drove him further along the road of moral disintegration. Haunted by fear and suspicion, he embarked in 1564 on a social revolution which in many features resembled the Totalitarianism of the twentieth century.

The Tsar divided the country into two parts; he retained control over only one of them, which he called " Oprichinna ". This word means in Russian a portion of property belonging to a widow or an orphan, and by choosing this name the Tsar wanted to show that he was nothing more than the helpless prey of his numerous secret enemies. All the leading posts in the districts assigned to " Oprichinna " were given to men called " the Oprichniki ". Anybody could join their ranks, regardless of race, religion or social origin. The only condition required was the readiness of the recruit to pledge himself to complete obedience to the Tsar, to execute faithfully all his orders, disregarding any moral objections they might provoke. The Oprichniki received special black uniforms, they rode on black horses and carried at their saddle-bow a dog's head and broom as symbols of their determination to guard, day and night, the safety of their master and to sweep away all his enemies. The Oprichniki were not allowed to mix with the common people. No family links and no social contacts between them and the rest of the population were tolerated. They were a law unto themselves; whenever an Oprichnik had a clash with an ordinary civilian he was always right, and his opponent was always wrong.

In order to complete the segregation of the two parts of the country, Ivan appointed another Tsar, a Tartar prince, named Simeon, who was supposed to rule the unredeemed section of the Russian people. By taking this step Ivan wanted to show that he had no responsibility for the rest of the nation and regarded them as his enemies. The main target for his attack was the upper classes, especially the old landed families, which had retained a good deal of independence from the time when Russia was still divided into many self-governing principalities. With refined cruelty they were ejected from their estates, tortured and

executed, whilst their lands and all their personal belongings
were handed over to the international crowd of Oprichniki, who
comprised Tartars, Poles, Lithuanians and Germans. Out of
two hundred leading families not more than twenty survived
this purge, and even these were greatly depleted. The extermination was so thorough that not only the male members suffered,
but also women, children and servants.

The maniac Tsar did not, however, confine his animosity to
the upper classes. Sometimes entire cities were put on the black
list, and their inhabitants were either killed or deported. Utter
bewilderment seized the terror-stricken nation. No one could
ever have foreseen such a calamity as this—a Tsar's waging regular
war against his own law-abiding people with the help of international ruffians. Ivan himself explained that he was obliged
to act thus in self-defence and, with the skill of a born demagogue,
he tried to enlist the moral support of the lower classes by affirm-
ing that his victims were those men and women of the nobility
who abused their privileges and wealth and therefore deserved
punishment.

His drastic social revolution met with no organised opposition,
but, in the midst of general dismay and confusion, a man arose
who was not afraid to stand against the Tsar. This was St.
Philip, Metropolitan of Moscow (1566–68).

Philip was born in 1507; he belonged to an old Moscow
family of Kolychev who had served their princes faithfully for
generations. He entered the religious life as a young man and
chose for his abode the famous monastery of Solovetsk, founded
by the monks from Novgorod in 1436. He was soon elected
Abbot, and for eighteen years he conducted with wisdom and
determination the affairs of his large community, which was
situated near the Arctic circle on an island in the White Sea. He
was not only a man of spiritual integrity but, as often happened
with Russian monks, was also endowed with outstanding practical sense. He was a skilled engineer, and a remarkable system
of irrigation, invented by him, turned the marshy soil of the
island into excellent grazing fields. Till the Communist Revolution of 1918, which transformed the monastery into one of the
most dreaded concentration camps, cattle-breeding and milk
products constituted the main sources of income for the monks
with their numerous visitors.

In 1565, Philip was summoned to Moscow, where a National

Assembly was held. There were two main topics for delibera-
tion—the discussion of the terms of a peace treaty with Poland
and the choice of a candidate for the Metropolitan See of Moscow.
Ivan was full of strange contradictions. He had several prelates
who were ready to say nothing against his conduct, but he
despised them and wanted to see as Metropolitan a man of holiness and integrity. The Assembly accordingly suggested German,
a famous missionary bishop who had dedicated his life to the conversion of the Tartars to the Christian faith. German, however,
made it clear that he was uncompromisingly opposed to Oprichinna. Ivan flew into a rage and expelled the old bishop from
Moscow. The next candidate was Philip. At first, he also refused
the office, but after long negotiations he accepted it and even
consented to raise no objections to " Oprichinna ", retaining,
however, the customary right of a Russian bishop to plead for the
victims of the Sovereign's displeasure (Pechalovanie). Philip
had no illusions about his ultimate fate; he interpreted his
elevation to the Metropolitan seat as a call to martyrdom. This
did not happen at once, however; there was to be a short respite.
Once again, the Tsar suddenly reformed his conduct, and for
two years peace reigned in Russia. Tortures and executions
were stopped, the prisons were emptied of their innocent victims,
and the country began to hope that Philip had achieved a
miracle and cured the Tsar of his maniacal obsessions. But this
return to sanity did not last long. In 1568, the Tsar relapsed
into his mood of vengeance and fear. Philip tried at first to
plead privately for the persecuted. His efforts having failed, he
decided to make use of a new weapon, never before employed in
the history of the Russian Church. He solemnly and publicly
rebuked the Tsar at a celebration of the Eucharist. The words
he addressed to the Sovereign were: " We are offering here the
pure, bloodless sacrifice for the salvation of men, but outside
this holy temple the blood of Christians is being shed and innocent people are being killed. Hast thou, Sire, forgotten that
thou, too, art dust and needest forgiveness of thy sins? Forgive,
and thou shalt be forgiven, for only if we forgive our subordinates
shall we escape divine condemnation. Thou hast deeply studied
the Holy Scriptures, and why hast thou not followed their
counsel? He who does not love his neighbour is not of God."
    Ivan was astounded, his presence of mind deserted him and
he fled from the church, overcome by fear and anger. In
revenge, he started a massacre of all those who were near and

dear to the daring bishop. Meanwhile, Philip himself remained unmolested. The Tsar was afraid to lay hands on him. He wanted first to deprive Philip of his episcopal dignity and afterwards to destroy him. In six months' time, he succeeded in convoking a Council. Its terrorised members unfrocked Philip on a charge of being guilty of black magic and immorality. Philip behaved with quiet dignity. He prophesied that his chief accuser, Pimen, the Metropolitan of Novgorod, would be summoned to God's impartial tribunal before him. This was fulfilled. Pimen perished at the Tsar's orders a few days later, after the closing of the Council. Philip himself was expelled from the capital and imprisoned in a monastery near Tver. He was strangled in his cell, on December 23rd, 1568, by Maluta Skuratov, the most hated of all the Oprichniki.

Philip was a martyr, who died, not as most martyrs have died, in defence of the faith, but in defence of Christian mercy, so flagrantly violated by the Tsar. He was not able to stop the massacre of innocent people, but he spoke as a Christian pastor in witness of the binding power of Christ's commandment over the ruler and the ruled. He does not stand alone; Russia has produced many men like him, but few of them have had the opportunity of raising their voices in such a manner that everybody could hear them. Yet they all performed the same service to the Christian cause as the famous Metropolitan, for they humbly and willingly sacrificed their lives to assert their belief in the truth of brotherly love and forgiveness.

The last years of Ivan's reign were a time of unredeemed misery. The Tsar sank ever deeper in his vices. In an attack of frenzied rage he killed his eldest son and heir (also named Ivan). The internal state of the country was chaotic; the enemies of Russia were everywhere triumphant. In 1571, the Tartars invaded Russia, and Moscow itself was sacked. In 1582, a humiliating peace with Poland was concluded. Ivan was obliged to renounce all the Russian territory which he had liberated in the first successful years of his reign. In 1583, he ceded to Sweden the entire Russian coast of the Baltic Sea. He died in 1584 at the age of fifty, exhausted both mentally and physically, leaving as his only heir a simpleton son named Theodor.

Russia has known many tyrannies, but never before or since have her people succumbed so completely and so helplessly to the arbitrary will of one man as during the long reign of Ivan the Terrible. Yet the nation was not lacking in men of strength and courage. The conquest of Siberia by a handful of Cossacks, the military successes in the first happy years when victories were scored against larger and better-equipped armies both in the East and in the West, the civil and ecclesiastical reforms and remarkable artistic achievements, all bear witness to the vigour and enterprise of the nation. The true reason for the lack of resistance to Ivan's campaign of terror has to be sought in the peculiar attitude to the Tsars commonly held by the Russians.

The Moscow principality was originally a small private estate belonging to its prince. All its inhabitants were his tenants, who stood in various degrees of dependence on the landlord, but who were free, when their obligations were fulfilled, to leave his domain and settle down in other parts of the country. During the reigns of Ivan and his immediate predecessors, Moscow grew into a great Empire, but the mentality of the princes and of the people did not change. The Tsars regarded themselves as the owners of the land, and all Russians called themselves their children and servants. When, for instance, the National Assemblies were convoked, they were not regarded as bodies representing the interests of different classes and defending their rights against the encroachments of the central power. The Assemblies were merely informal family gatherings where the Tsars could sound the opinion of the people, obtain, if necessary, their approval of new measures, and secure their collaboration. But the Tsars remained their own masters, and they were free to act either in accordance with or against the advice of the Assembly. Russians in the sixteenth century did not claim the right to share in the government of the country, but they considered themselves free to go away from the Moscow domain if they were discontented. This psychology was clearly revealed in the correspondence which took place between Ivan and Prince Kurbski. The latter was one of the best-educated men of his time. He was an able general, who had conducted several successful campaigns, but, when Ivan started the persecution of the landed aristocracy, Prince Kurbski fled to Lithuania and became there the leader of the Orthodox party. In letters addressed to the Tsar from abroad he bitterly attacked his former friend. However, he never questioned Ivan's right to do what he liked with his possessions and with their inhabitants as long as they remained settled on the Tsar's lands; he only accused Ivan of foolishness in persecuting his best servants and in surrounding himself with bad and greedy advisers. If a man of Kurbski's education and standing had no other idea of the Moscow State than that it was the private estate of the Tsar, even less could the rest of the people organise opposition to the Sovereign on political grounds. Only as Christians addressing the Tsar, who was also a Christian, could they raise their objections, and that was the reason why St. Philip's rebuke carried such moral weight.

Ivan treated all opponents of Oprichinna as rebels against his lawful power, but Philip could not be accused under this heading, for he did not raise any objection to Oprichinna as an institution, but to the morally wrong use of it. He spoke to Ivan as one Christian to another, and the Tsar had to invent fictitious charges against the daring bishop in order to stop him. Both Ivan and his victims were firmly convinced that God was the true Ruler of all nations and that to Him every man would one day give an account of his conduct. The Russians regarded Ivan as a punishment from above, inflicted upon them for their sins, and hoped that by God's mercy their sufferings would not last long, and this helped them to face their trials. Ivan had a lofty theory of the great power which, by divine providence, was given to the Tsars. He was profoundly convinced that he was the successor of the Byzantine Emperors, and his replies to Prince Kurbski's letters eloquently defended autocracy by theological arguments. But the only Empire he knew was that of the Mongols. Therefore, whenever he wanted to display his supreme power, he saw no better way than imitation of the Tartar Khans, who, in order to prove their might, used to inflict arbitrary punishments upon their best servants.

Ivan was the first Russian revolutionary. He inspired and carried through that special type of revolution directed by the head of the State which has since become a characteristic feature of Russian history. He used his high authority as a divine sanction for the brutal treatment of all those who stood for the traditional order. By doing so he undermined the organic growth of Russian culture and prepared the ground for the violence of Peter the Great's reforms in the eighteenth century and for the Red Terror of the Communist experiment of the twentieth. He was, however, not solely responsible for this tragic turn in the history of Russia, for his whole outlook was shaped by the teaching of the Possessors. Their theory of the Tsar's illimitable power contributed much to Ivan's abuse of the authority acquired by him over the Russian people.

Bitter was the experience which the leaders of that party brought upon the nation, but the Russians survived the anguish and revealed some of their best qualities during the reign of Theodor, the last Tsar of the House of Rurik.

CHAPTER VIII

TSAR THEODOR AND THE ESTABLISHMENT OF THE PATRIARCHATE IN MOSCOW

THEODOR was twenty-seven years old when he inherited his father's throne (1584). Small in stature, shy and retiring, with a vague smile always playing over his pale face, he seemed to be quite unfit both mentally and physically to carry the burden of government of his vast Empire. Foreign envoys described the new Tsar as an ordinary idiot, and they believed that his reign would soon end in disaster. The nation was deeply disturbed by the revolution carried through by Ivan, and it seemed that only an exceptionally able statesman could avert political and social collapse. Contrary to all these forebodings, the fourteen years of Theodor's reign were a period of unprecedented progress and prosperity. The country enjoyed internal peace; its frontiers were considerably enlarged both in the southern and eastern directions, and even in the west several Russian towns lost to the Swedes were recovered. But, above all, the greatest ambition of the Russians was at last fulfilled—the Metropolitan of Moscow was elevated to the status of Patriarch.

The secret of Theodor's success lay in the special appeal which his personality made to his people. He satisfied some of their deepest aspirations and thus provided them with a sense of unity and strength. For eight hundred years his family had ruled over Russia. Theodor's ancestors had all been absorbed in the struggle for power. Their heroism, virtues and sacrifices had brought glory and success to the country; their crimes, foolishness and egoism had caused misery and suffering to millions of other human beings. Theodor, the last representative of the House of Rurik, displayed a complete detachment from all earthly concerns. He was brought up amidst orgies and executions, frequently relieved by long Church services through which Ivan tried to appease his guilty conscience. The boy was disliked by his father and ill-treated by the courtiers, and yet, in spite of this appalling upbringing, he was neither polluted nor embittered. He grew up into a man of childlike simplicity and

65

candour, of pure heart and mind, whose sole interest was centred in divine worship. His life was the very denial of worldliness, and he remained quite unmoved by the passion for earthly possessions which played such a prominent part in the life of his father and forefathers. There was, however, nothing gloomy or morbid about Theodor. He loved art, beauty and fun. He was deeply attached to his wife, and he could spend long hours at Church services, fascinated by the splendour and mystery of their eternal drama. He was weak in body, simple in mind, but sound in his religion and moral judgment. Indifferent to the ordinary routine of administration, he left it in the hands of his advisers, first among whom was his gifted brother-in-law, Boris Godunov. But there was one sphere of government in which his will was felt. This simpleton, robed in gorgeous vestments, was determined that bloodshed, cruelty and oppression must be stopped, and it was stopped as long as he occupied the throne of his ancestors.

Theodor was not an ordinary idiot; he was one of the " fools in Christ ", whom the Russians believe to be under God's special protection. Some of these " fools " are born defective; others deliberately take upon themselves this extreme form of self-denial. They seem to be the most useless members of human society, yet they perform a significant service: they demonstrate that God is stronger than man, and that a helpless and despised human being, if he trusts in divine love and protection, can achieve greater things than a clever but self-centred person. These " fools in Christ " (iurodivy) are known all over Russia; they go from one village to another, barefoot, dressed in rags, yet enduring with immunity the snow and the freezing wind of Russian winters. They are kept warm by some unknown power which is outside the control of ordinary men.

The presence of such a " fool " on the throne of Russia brought comfort and consolation to the nation deeply stricken by the terror of Ivan's reign.[1] The Russians knew that their

[1] A contemporary document entitled " A brief description of the Moscow Tsars, of their appearance, age, habits and disposition " contains the following portraits of Ivan the Terrible and his son Theodor, which display clearly the attitude of the Russians to these two rulers :—

" The Tsar Ivan was of unattractive appearance, with grey eyes and a long hooked nose. He was tall and muscular with a lean dry body, high shouldered and broad chested. He was a man of unusual behaviour. He was versed in book learning and very eloquent ; fierce in attack, and strong in defence of his

Tsar was not able to rule over them properly, but they were sure that he could pray and that his prayers, his childlike simplicity and faith, his very helplessness and profound humility were their shield and protection and a source of sanctification for the whole nation. Russia was a family, the Tsar was the father, the head of the body, and the fact that he was near to God and beloved by Him meant that all Russians shared in this grace. The masses of Russian people, crude and uncivilised, often debased and immoral, were uplifted by the thought that, whilst they were sunk in their iniquities, their Tsar was praying for them and bearing the burden of their corporate sin. Often in the early hours of the morning the inhabitants of Moscow were awakened from sleep by the deep sound of the great Kremlin bells, and they knew that their Tsar was personally calling his people to prayer, for Theodor was specially skilled in the art of bell-ringing. The Russians were convinced that God would show His mercy to the nation which obeyed its helpless Sovereign. They rejoiced to think that their country was so trusted by God that He had committed to Theodor's feeble but gentle hands the destiny of millions of Russian people.

It was therefore not an accident that during his reign the Russian Church reached the status of a patriarchate and took a position of prominence among other Eastern Christians. Since the adoption by the Grand Princes of Moscow of the title of Tsar, the Russians had longed to see the patriarchal throne established in Moscow. Tradition required that the Emperor should be anointed by the Patriarch, and the absence of the latter in Russia was a challenge to the claims of her Tsars to be the successors of the Byzantine Basileus.

Many obstacles, however, stood in the way of the realisation

---

patrimony. He was very hard-hearted in the treatment of his subjects, given to him by God, daring and hasty to shed blood, and pitiless. He destroyed large numbers of his people, both great and small. During his reign many cities he burned, many clergy he imprisoned and without mercy condemned to death, women and girls he polluted with fornication, and many other evil things he committed against his subjects. The same Tsar Ivan did also many good things : he cared greatly for the army and, without sparing, gave to it all that it needed. Such was the Tsar Ivan.

" The Tsar Theodor was small of stature, and bore the marks of fasting. He was humble, given to the things of the soul, constant in prayer, liberal in alms ; for the things of the world he did not care, but only for the salvation of the soul. From childhood till the very end of his life he lived thus. God crowned his reign with peace, put down his enemies beneath his feet and granted good and restful times, because of his salutary works. Such was the Tsar Theodor."

of this wish. The Russians, with their innate respect for Church tradition, did not want to act in a revolutionary manner. They desired, therefore, the consent of the Eastern prelates; but the Greeks, who tenaciously clung to their ecclesiastical supremacy, insisted that the number of four ancient patriarchates was sacred and sealed for ever and that no new patriarch could be added to it. The Russians, however, won the battle and, by a skilful manœuvre, not only obtained the approval of the change by all Eastern hierarchs, but even secured the Greek signature to the document, which expressed in a most solemn manner the belief in Moscow as the Third and Last Rome. The events which led to this victory were as follows :—

In 1588, the Patriarch of Constantinople, Jeremiah, came to Moscow in quest of alms. It was the first time that a senior hierarch of the Eastern Church had visited Russia. He was greeted with pomp and many festivities. He was greatly impressed with the splendour of the Church services and the devotion of the people. The Russians took the opportunity of his stay to re-open negotiations about the patriarchate and, in order to overcome the usual methods of Oriental diplomacy, with its non-committal promises and indefinite postponements, made a drastic proposal. They invited Jeremiah himself to become the patriarch of the Russian Church. It was a tempting offer for a man who led a precarious existence as the head of Christians under the Turks. Here in Russia, he was treated as a beloved father in God; honour and popular devotion were offered to him. In Turkey, he was held responsible for every act committed by the Christians and lived in constant danger of martyrdom. After prolonged discussions, Jeremiah gave his consent. By so doing, he recognised at last the right of Russia to have her own patriarchs. This was immediately recorded and retreat from that position was made impossible. But, once this was achieved, the Russians began to limit the scope of their original proposal by adding new conditions which made it much less attractive. They explained that they were unable to dismiss the present occupant of the metropolitan seat of Moscow, Job, from his post, and they offered to the Greek prelate a seat in the provincial city of Vladimir. Other difficulties, such as those of language and differences in customs and tradition, were raised. The Greek prelate discovered meanwhile many inconveniences in Russian life which he had not noticed at first. The climate was cold, the food heavy and unusual, the services extremely long and exhausting, and the patriarch was expected to set an example of endurance and piety.

So, after further protracted negotiations, Jeremiah himself suggested that a Russian might, after all, be a more suitable candidate for the patriarchal seat. This was exactly what the Russian Government wanted, and, thus, on January 26th, 1589, eighteen months after Jeremiah had arrived in the Russian capital, he himself elevated Job, the Metropolitan of Moscow, to the dignity of Patriarch of all Russia. In the installation charter, signed by Jeremiah, the following was inserted: " Because the old Rome has collapsed on account of the heresy of Apollinarius,[1] and because the second Rome, which is Constantinople, is now in possession of the godless Turks, thy great kingdom, O pious Tsar, is the third Rome. It surpasses in devotion every other, and all Christian kingdoms are now merged in thy realm. Thou art the only Christian sovereign in the world, the master of all faithful Christians." This sentence was an almost verbatim reproduction of Philotheus' epistle to Basil III. A century earlier it was the daring prophecy of a devout monk; now it was a solemn declaration made by the highest authority of the Eastern Church.

It is open to question whether Jeremiah himself fully understood the Russian text and shared the interpretation given by the Russians to the act committed by him. The events of the next century revealed that the Greeks and the Russians differed considerably in their attitude to Moscow's claims. But, in the sixteenth century, there was nothing as yet to disturb the peace between them. Jeremiah returned to Constantinople carrying with him generous alms and promising to secure the recognition of his action by the remaining three patriarchs of the East.

This was not a very easy matter, but, after four years of persistent effort, during which gifts were liberally distributed among the Eastern prelates, the Russians at last won the desired approval. It was granted in 1593, when all four patriarchs met in Constantinople and offered to their new brother in Moscow the fifth and last place in the hierarchy of honour. Such a decision conflicted with the charter signed by Jeremiah in Moscow four years

---

[1] The use of unleavened bread in the Eucharist by the Latins was interpreted by the Russians as a sign of a defective conception of the Incarnation, leavened bread representing for them the fullness of manhood in Christ.

earlier. The Russians were discontented, they wanted to secure at least the third place for their patriarch, but they had to be satisfied with the major concession which had given them a patriarchal seat without causing a breach in relations with the conservative heads of the Eastern Church.

The ecclesiastical victory attained by the Russians completed the edifice of the Moscow Tsardom, and they ascribed their success to the prayers of their pious sovereign. It had taken them just a century to provide their liberated land with both Tsar and Patriarch, but the place occupied by them in the life of Russia was different from that which had belonged to their namesakes in Byzantium. A Patriarch of Constantinople had extensive and well-defined canonical powers. He was the head of a large ecclesiastical province with many metropolitans and archbishops under his jurisdiction. The elevation of the Moscow metropolitan to the same dignity did not convey similar privileges. This was achieved at a time when the party of Possessors controlled the life of the Russian Church and imposed upon the new institution the imprint of their interpretation of Christianity.

The hierarch's advance from the status of metropolitan to that of patriarch had no effect upon the jurisdiction of the See. The Patriarch of all Russia was in reality an ordinary diocesan bishop. He was the senior and most influential among them, but he never had any special powers over the rest of the episcopate. It was in the sphere of worship and Church ceremonial that the glory and power of his new title were fully revealed to the nation. With great love, the Russians provided their senior hierarch with gorgeous robes and amplified the services by introducing parts which only the Patriarch was entitled to perform. The relations between the Tsar and the Patriarch were left undefined. They were entirely family-like and unofficial. The Patriarch might have considerable influence in State affairs, or he might be reduced to complete insignificance: it all depended on his personal contacts with the sovereign. The Patriarch was treated as the man whose duty it was to offer prayers on behalf of the whole nation. His main functions were liturgical and not juridical. In some ways he resembled the High Priest of the Old Testament rather than the ecclesiastical dignitary of the Christianised Roman Empire.

The story of the establishment of the Moscow Patriarchate illustrates the spiritual growth of the nation. Only a hundred years before, the Russians had been an enslaved people; by the sixteenth century they had become the builders of a great realm, fully conscious of their religious mission. The new house they were erecting was planned on a solid and permanent foundation, and they were not in a hurry. They were careful, therefore, to maintain the connection with the Eastern Patriarchates which were all that was left of the ancient glory of Byzantium. An Eastern prelate in the sixteenth century was only a poor beggar whose life depended on the mercy of Turkish officials, but he was invested with spiritual authority of great antiquity, and for this he was honoured by the Russian Christians.

Russians were backward in technical matters, their manners were often crude, but they held a sound scale of values and had a profound respect for tradition. The people were endowed with a genuine sense of their corporate membership in the Church. This was demonstrated during the crucial years which followed the extinction of the old dynasty.

CHAPTER IX

THE TIME OF TROUBLES

In the early morning of January 7th, 1598, Theodor Ivanovich, the Tsar of all Russia, passed peacefully away. With his death, the House of Rurik, which had ruled the country from the beginning of its history, came to an end. As the Russian Tsars were the sole owners of the whole land, the divinely appointed heads of the family, the idea of electing a monarch was quite foreign to the Russian mind. Everyone felt lost. The first reaction of the people was to ask Irina, Theodor's widow, to take upon herself the government. Since the time of Princess Olga (*d*. 969), there had been no women rulers in Russia, but in these exceptional circumstances the nation unanimously recognised the Tsaritsa as the Sovereign. Irina firmly refused, however, to accept responsibility and retired to a convent. In despair, the people turned to the newly-elected Patriarch, Job, asking him for his advice. They realised that at this time, when their traditional order was falling to pieces, the spiritual authority of the Patriarch remained the only force that could keep the nation together. Job responded to this call. He sent out invitations to all parts of the country asking the population to dispatch their representatives to Moscow. A National Assembly was gathered, and, at the Patriarch's suggestion, Boris Godunov was invited to become the Tsar of all Russia. He at first declined the honour, but under the threat of ecclesiastical punishment he finally consented and was crowned on September 1st, 1598, in the Cathedral Church of the Assumption. His reign opens the period of Russian history known as " the Time of Troubles ".

There was a strange contrast between Theodor's rule and that of Boris. Theodor seemed to lack all the qualifications necessary for a good Sovereign; Boris had most of them; and yet it was Boris who was the complete failure, and Theodor the success. It is difficult to imagine two men with gifts and limitations in greater contrast than theirs. Boris was brilliant, handsome, eloquent and energetic—a skilful diplomat and an accomplished administrator. He had the right ideas and he knew how to put them into practice. Theodor looked particularly helpless in the presence of his brother-in-law, who was so full of vitality and ambition; but he had a knowledge of truth which was outside the reach of the self-seeking Boris.

The Godunovs were of Tartar origin, and Boris possessed the secretiveness, the self-control and the revengefulness of the Mongol. He was mistrustful of all, and no one in the country trusted him. He rose to power during the reign of Ivan the Terrible, among whose debased accomplices he appeared sober, intelligent and attractive. He himself practised neither cruelty nor vice, but he did not condemn those who indulged in them. Ivan became greatly attached to young Boris, and the youth, with supreme skill, kept the Tsar's favour till the end. He was also the only courtier who showed respect and kindness to the simpleton Theodor, and it was his plan to marry his beautiful sister, Irina, to the helpless prince.

It was natural that, when, against all expectation, Theodor became Tsar of Russia, Boris should assume full control of home and foreign affairs, and he invariably conducted them with success. When, therefore, he himself ascended to the Russian throne he had every reason to believe that his reign would be crowned with glory. But this did not happen, and the eight years of his rule constituted one long series of disasters. It started with a famine (1601–3), one of the worst in Russian history, and, during the disorders which resulted from it, the striking news spread suddenly all over the country that Boris was, after all, only a usurper, for yet another representative of the House of Rurik was still alive.

There is still much unresolved mystery about the man who challenged Boris by calling himself Tsarevich Dmitri. This was the name of Ivan's son, born of his fifth wife, Maria Nagaia. The boy perished in strange circumstances on May 15th, 1591, when he was nine years old, and for a time he was forgotten. But during the famine his name reappeared on the scene of Russian life, and for nine years the country lived under its charm. The story of Prince Dmitri is one of the most dramatic episodes in Russian history, full of absorbing psychological interest. No one knows the origin of the Pretender who ruled Russia from 1605 to 1606, under the name of Tsar Dmitri Ivanovich; and the identity has not been discovered of yet another man who, under the same name, Dmitri, raised a mighty rebellion in 1608, and for two years threatened Moscow from his capital at Tushino.

The widespread support which these pretenders received from Russian people, and the failure which befell Boris's, and later Tsar Basil's, attempt to check their advance, are further illustrations of the moral foundation on which Russian national solidarity was built in the fifteenth and sixteenth centuries.

Life in Russia was hard. The defence of the country required heavy sacrifices from everyone, and every class had to carry its own burden of responsibility People had little notion of rights and privileges but a strong sense of obligation to the community. In this they were supported by the conviction that every man was assigned by God his own particular type of service. The idea of deliberate attempts to attain greater power, to seek through skill or cunning a more advantageous position, was repugnant to the Russian mind, for it implied the imposition of a still heavier burden upon those members of the same group who were left behind. The Tsars were obeyed not because they were better or stronger than others, but because they belonged to the family of Rurik, which was appointed by God to rule over the nation.

The case of Ivan the Terrible was a typical one. He was a bad man, but the Russians nevertheless obeyed him till the end. The nation regarded his reign of terror as a divine chastisement, and the people felt that their Tsar was as much the prey of evil as were his helpless victims. Ivan could sink deep in cruelty and vice, but he suffered acutely, and there were times when he burned with shame and horror at his own misdeeds. These instances of repentance constituted a moral link between him and the other Christians of Russia.

With Boris, everything was different. He was sober, self-controlled; he was not carried away by his passions; he wanted to promote the good of the people. But the main motive behind his actions was his lust for power, and therefore he was profoundly distrusted by the nation. The Russians became convinced that Boris would, in cold blood, commit any crime if it suited his designs, and this gave rise to the belief that he had cunningly prepared the way for his own accession to the throne, by murdering Prince Dmitri, an innocent and helpless boy. The Russians felt by instinct that Boris either had actually broken, or was ready to break, the bond of moral solidarity which united them all, and therefore as soon as the news was heard that Dmitri was alive, everyone interpreted it as a sign of divine punishment inflicted upon the ambitious and unscrupulous climber. These deep-rooted suspicions were not without foundation, for in the critical moment of his life Boris entirely lost his usual self-control. He behaved like a man haunted by fear and remorse. He began to inflict ill-directed blows upon real and imaginary enemies and started a campaign of terror, similar to that from which the country suffered during Ivan's reign. In the midst of this desperate struggle he suddenly collapsed and died on April 13th, 1605.

He had lost the battle. He was defeated, however, not by the Pretender and those of his enemies who engineered the plot, but by the Russian people themselves, who were resolutely opposed to that aggressive and amoral individualism of which Boris was such a brilliant and accomplished exponent.

A few months after Boris's death, the man who called himself Dmitri triumphantly entered Moscow, being enthusiastically welcomed by the people, who believed that he was a true son of the House of Rurik. For eleven months Russia was ruled by this stranger; he was short, red-haired, clumsy in his manners, but he acted with the supreme confidence of a man who knows himself to be a born sovereign. Though he was a pure Russian, he started his campaign from Poland, and his supporters were mostly recruited from among the Lithuanians and Poles, and this contributed to his undoing. Many of these foreigners came to Moscow, and their presence irritated the local population. The leading boiars, who resented the independent behaviour and democratic bearing of the new Tsar, organised a plot against him which cost him his life.

The leader of the new revolution was the boiarin Basil Shuiski and he was proclaimed Tsar by his followers (1606-10). His accession to the throne represented an attempt of the leading Moscow families to establish a rule of aristocracy like that which existed in Poland and Lithuania. They wanted to secure their own privileged position at the expense of the rest of the people, but this plan failed completely. The nation refused to obey a Tsar who was a nominee of one class only, and the country was plunged into civil war. Another Pretender, also calling himself Dmitri, established his headquarters near Moscow, at Tushino, and directed from there a regular campaign against the Tsar Basil. Meanwhile Poles, Swedes and Cossacks invaded Russia, adding greatly to the general anarchy.

The climax of national calamity was reached in 1610, when Basil Shuiski was forced to abdicate. After his fall there was no longer anyone responsible for the order and unity of the land. The Poles captured Smolensk, the fortress that guarded the road to Moscow. Novgorod was seized by the Swedes; and the boiars in Moscow, terrified by the peasants' rebellion which swept across all provinces, elected Wladyslaw, a young son of Sigismund III, King of Poland (d. 1632), as Tsar, and opened the gates of the Kremlin to a Polish garrison.

At this time of complete moral collapse, when no one knew who was his friend or his foe, when everyone cared only for his own interest, and when, therefore, everybody suffered acutely, the country was once more saved by the Church. Its faithful members were the only section of the people who retained their sense of responsibility for the whole of the nation and were ready to sacrifice themselves for the common good. Of the large number of outstanding Christians who contributed to the restoration of peace and order, only a few names can be mentioned here: such, for instance, as St. Germogen, the Patriarch of Moscow (1606–12); St. Dionisi, the Archimandrite, and Avraami, the bursar, both of the Monastery of the Holy Trinity of Radonezh; Kusma Minin-Sukhoruk and St. Juliania Ossorgina of Lazorevsk.

Germogen was seventy-six years old when, during Basil Shuiski's reign, he was elected to the patriarchal throne in 1606, and for six stormy years he stood firm as a rock amidst the general confusion, treachery and anarchy of his time. It was a period of Russian history when those who occupied posts of high responsibility were ready to sell their country together with their honour, when patriotism was dead and every crime seemed to be lawful. The old Patriarch, who had spent his long life as a humble parish priest in the provincial town of Kazan, remained unperturbed and steadfast. He did not belong to any party and advocated no particular political programme; he appealed to the moral conscience of the people, imploring them to repent of their sins, to begin again to obey the divine commandments and to unite in their efforts to restore freedom and order in their motherland.

After Basil's abdication in 1610, Germogen became a virtual

prisoner of the Poles, who kept him under close guard within the walls of the Kremlin. But they were not able to silence him. His pastoral epistles were secretly dispatched to all parts of the country, and they brought hope and consolation to his faithful flock. He was the symbol of national unity, an inspiring example of a man who served a good cause regardless of the cost. The Poles, seeing that they were unable to stop his activities, starved the old bishop to death, but this crime did not bring them much profit. Other bishops and Church leaders stepped into his place, the most influential among them being the Archimandrite Dionisi and his friend, Avraami Palitsyn. They were the heads of the House of the Holy Trinity, founded by St. Sergius of Radonezh. It had always been a centre of religious and national unity for Russian people, but in " the Time of Troubles " it rose to the position of an impregnable stronghold of Russia's independence.

The Polish army, 30,000 strong, was sent to take control of the fortified monastery, but the monks, inspired by their trust in the prayers of their founder, refused to surrender. For sixteen long months they stood the siege; many of them died from wounds and starvation, but they were victorious. The Poles were forced to retreat. This success deeply impressed the whole country, and evoked in the people the desire to be free from the foreign invaders.

The man who gave shape and direction to the patriotic movement was a churchwarden of one of the parishes of Nizhni Novgorod, named Kusma Minin-Sukhoruk, a butcher by trade. He saw in a dream St. Sergius of Radonezh, who ordered him to organise the army of liberation. When the same vision was repeated, Minin started to act. His first appeal was addressed to his own parish. He sold all that he possessed in order to raise the money for the equipment of the soldiers, and he asked others to follow his example. His fellow parishioners responded, and Nizhni Novgorod, this important city on the Volga, became the centre of national revival. Other towns imitated its example. Prince Pozharski, an experienced general, was selected as military leader, whilst Minin retained control over finance and administration, displaying outstanding ability in the exercise of his duties.

The new army started its operations in the autumn of 1611; by March 1612, the Russians had cleared the provinces along the Upper Volga of the Polish and Cossack bands; on August 10th, the forces of liberation reached Moscow, which was still held by the Poles. The latter, after a desperate fight, were obliged to surrender the city to Minin and Pozharski on November 29th, 1612.

As soon as the capital was recovered from the enemy, a National Assembly was convoked, which in 1613 elected Michael Romanov, a youth of sixteen, as the Tsar of all Russia, and this was the end of " the Time of Troubles ".

The speed with which the Russians were able to recover from their mortal illness was a proof of the health of the national organism. The success of a man like Minin or Avraami Palitsyn, who acted as chaplain to the Army of Liberation, was due to the presence of a large number of sound Christians in all sections of society.

St. Juliania Ossorgina can serve as an example of those innumerable Christian men and women whose faith and love made possible the quick recuperation of the nation. Her biography, composed by her son, gives us a vivid picture of an outstanding Christian. She is one of the few canonised women who were neither martyrs nor nuns. She was the wife of a well-to-do and important official, the mother of thirteen children and the mistress of a large household. Her husband was often away from home on government service, and Juliania was busy all the day with running her family estate. She was efficient and popular with her relatives and servants. But when her day's duties were over, she gave her nights to prayer and needlework. She was a great artist, and the money which she earned with her own hands she spent on the poor, the sick and the orphans. She was severe with herself and gentle with all those who asked her assistance. She mortified her flesh like the Eastern ascetics, walking in the Russian winter without stockings and abstaining from food for days; but she did it to make herself better able to serve all those who were in need of her help. In the dreadful years of the great famine (1601–3), she gave away to the starving people all that she possessed, and then when her food supply was exhausted she began to collect herbs and roots. In her able hands these unpalatable substitutes for ordinary food became nourishing and tasty, and in this way she saved the lives of hundreds of people. She died after a short illness on January 2nd, 1604. She was canonised soon after her death, so deep was the impression of holiness and integrity which she produced upon all those who came in contact with her. Juliania could neither read nor write, but she knew Christ and she loved Him only; she wanted to be a nun, but, in obedience to her family, she married and led the life of her class and status. In each man and woman she met, she served her Divine Master. This was the source of her overflowing charity and of her surprising endurance; for no sacrifice was hard for her if it could alleviate the pain suffered by another creature made in the image of her Lord. This profound devotion to the Saviour made her a shining light in the dark years of struggle and confusion in which she lived and died. Christians like Juliania Ossorgina were the salt of Russia. The country could face any trial or danger as long as it could rely upon their labours and prayers.

The Time of Troubles was the last stage of the social revolution initiated by Ivan the Terrible. By his indiscriminate use of violence, he weakened the moral solidarity of the nation and let loose class rivalries and the dark passions always lurking in human souls. The Church was, however, the force which helped the Russians to overcome these temptations and to restore their unity and vigour.

The upheaval of those fateful years throws a valuable light upon the inner structure of Russian life: it shows that the Russians, being corporate-minded, are always at their best when they act under their own elected leaders and live in self-governing communities. These conditions were more adequately reproduced in the north-eastern provinces in the sixteenth and seventeenth centuries than in other parts of the country, and this is why Nizhni Novgorod and the neighbouring towns became the centres of national revival. Minin, the leader of the movement of liberation, was so successful because he expressed the mind and the will of thousands of his fellow-countrymen. He was not seeking any profit for himself, his only desire being to serve the community, and as soon as he had accomplished his task he retired to his previous position as an ordinary citizen.

The unity of the Russian people was neither political nor racial; its foundation was religious, and this was clearly demonstrated in the Time of Troubles. When its moral basis was undermined, first by Ivan, and later by Boris and the Moscow boiars, the entire country was plunged into anarchy, but as soon as the Christian conscience was awakened, peace and order were restored and the nation started work with renewed zeal on the rebuilding of its badly damaged home.

CHAPTER X

THE ORTHODOX IN POLAND AND LITHUANIA

WHILE the Russians under the Moscow Tsardom were growing in national strength and unity, and this in spite of their failures and setbacks, a different destiny befell those of them who found themselves incorporated in Lithuania and Poland. The first great landmark in their history was the conversion of the Grand Prince of Lithuania, Yagailo (d. 1434), to Roman Catholicism, in 1386.[1] The events which led to this conversion were as follows:—

King Kasimir of Poland died in 1370, leaving no heir. This meant that King Luis the Great of Hungary inherited all his domains, including Russian Galicia, in accordance with the treaty concluded between these two monarchs in 1352.[2] King Luis died in 1382, and, having no sons, he bequeathed his vast dominion to two of his daughters. The eldest, Maria, became Queen of Hungary; the youngest, Jadwiga, who was only fifteen years old, was made Queen of Poland, whilst the fate of Galicia remained undecided. The position of Poland at that time was more than precarious, for it was threatened by Germany and Lithuania, and had also to cope with the unruly aristocracy and discontented Orthodox population of the newly acquired Russian provinces. The country needed a strong ruler, and a fifteen-year-old Hungarian girl was obviously little suited for this rôle. At this critical moment, the Poles decided to ask Yagailo, the Grand Prince of the powerful State of Lithuania, to marry Jadwiga, and thus become king of both countries. The only condition attached to this proposal was his joining the Roman Catholic Church. Yagailo gladly consented. He was a member of the Orthodox Church, but he was re-baptized and re-confirmed and duly married in 1386 to Jadwiga, whose previous marriage to William of Austria was annulled.

It was not an easy task to amalgamate the two countries. The majority of the Lithuanians were Orthodox, and they, together with the large Russian population, resented the King's

---

[1] See Chapter IV, page 30.   [2] See Chapter IV, pages 28-9

change of religion. Yagailo tried at first to force the Lithuanians to follow his example, but, threatened by rebellion, he
gave up these efforts. He settled down in Poland, leaving the
government of his Russo-Lithuanian lands in the able hands of
his cousin Vitovt (*d.* 1430), who also became a Roman Catholic
but showed no desire for proselytism. This was the beginning
of an order which lasted for two hundred years: Poland and
Lithuania remained independent states having each their own
government, finance and army, but they were ruled by the same
dynasty, and this link kept the two realms together.

The Eastern Christians formed the vast majority in Lithuania.
At the beginning of the fifteenth century there were seven
million Orthodox and one million Roman Catholics there, but
the Orthodox laboured under the serious disadvantage of being
ruled by a Roman Catholic dynasty which used all possible
means for encouraging Latin Christianity at the expense of the
Eastern tradition. The Lithuanian princes readily granted to
the aristocracy extensive privileges over the peasants, such as the
nobles enjoyed in Roman Catholic Poland and Hungary. These
privileges were, however, accompanied by a request that the gentry
should submit to the Pope (such were, for instance, the terms of
the agreement signed by Yagailo and Vitovt in 1413 at Gorodok).

Both in Poland and in Hungary the Church was identified
with Latin culture, an exotic plant in those remote eastern
corners of Europe and therefore more highly valued there than
anywhere else. The Polish gentry went so far as to use Latin
in Parliament and at Court, and they despised all those who
were not familiar with that language. This attitude of mind
created a wider gap between the aristocracy and the common
people in Poland than in any other European country, by giving
all rights to the nobility, and none to the peasantry.

The Grand Princes of Lithuania, by gradually introducing
the same order into their land, separated the upper from the
lower classes and thus considerably undermined the strength
of the Orthodox opposition. Another weapon used by them
against the Eastern Church was the appointment to episcopal
sees of men of feeble character and unworthy life. The fruits of
this policy of weakening and dividing Eastern Orthodoxy were
reaped at the end of the sixteenth century, when a group of
Orthodox bishops went over to Rome.

" The Unia " of 1596 marks intensification of the long

struggle between Latin and Eastern Christians under Lithuanian and Polish rule. The ground was prepared during the
reign of Sigismund Augustus (1548-72), the last king of the
Yagellon dynasty. He was the most tolerant of all Polish and
Lithuanian rulers, and it was owing to his popularity that he
succeeded in achieving a permanent union between the two
countries. The treaty of Lublin, concluded in 1569, made
Poland and Lithuania one State, ruled by one elected monarch;
but the only class which had the right to elect the king was the
gentry, whilst the peasantry was reduced to a state of complete
enslavement. The Russian lands of Kiev, Podolia and Volhynia,
according to terms of the Treaty, were incorporated in Poland
and came under more vigorous Roman Catholic control. The
Treaty of Lublin inaugurated a period of determined attacks
upon the Orthodox Church, which were conducted this time by
the Jesuits. They first appeared in Poland in 1560, their original
intention being to combat Lutheranism and Calvinism, which
had secured large followings among the aristocracy and the city
population. Soon, however, the Jesuits turned their attention
to the Orthodox Church. In 1570, they founded a College in
Vilno for the sons of the Russian and Lithuanian aristocracy,
and this proved to be one of their most efficient weapons. It
was the best school in the country, and it was soon filled with
keen and gifted young men. They entered the Academy with
different religious and national backgrounds, but after nine years
of intense training they all left it as ardent supporters of the
Roman cause. Special circumstances favoured this desertion of
their Mother Church by the Orthodox aristocracy.

At the end of the sixteenth century the Eastern Church was
passing through a particularly difficult period. The Christians
in Constantinople, the Balkans, Asia Minor, Egypt and Syria
were reduced by the Mahometans to a pitiful state. They had
no schools, no printing press; their laity was ignorant, their
priests were poor and badly trained. The Church of Russia, the
only free branch of Eastern Christianity, was at the mercy of a
maniac Tsar who was deliberately destroying the few educated
men the country possessed. Everywhere in the East was fear
and oppression; while Western Christians, stimulated by the
Reformation and Counter-Reformation, were full of vigour, zeal
and learning. Besides, an Orthodox nobleman, as soon as he

left his Church, was immediately admitted as an equal into the brilliant society of the Polish aristocracy, and at the same time he acquired still greater power over his peasants.

All these considerations rapidly reduced the numbers of the Orthodox gentry, but their conversion did not solve the problem of the schism, for the bulk of the Eastern Christians clung tenaciously to their Church and showed no intention of going over to Rome. In order to win them, the Jesuits designed an ingenious plan of creating a new type of Churchmanship, Eastern in its worship and ceremonial, but Papal in its allegiance and in the spirit of its discipline. This was the so-called " Uniate Church ". The first step in the execution of the scheme was to win over the Episcopate of the Orthodox Church.

The Russian bishops under Polish rule were mostly recruited from wealthy families; few of them had either the training or the moral qualifications required for their office. Many of them looked with envy upon the privileged position enjoyed by Roman Catholic prelates. The latter were members of the Senate, lived in palaces and had large revenues. They were also indisputable masters in their own dioceses. The position of the Orthodox bishops was different. They had no political status, they were supposed to be monks and were therefore expected to live a humble and simple life; finally, they had to share the government of their dioceses with the laity and the parochial clergy. Skilfully exploiting the bishops' discontent, the Jesuits promised them equal political rights with the Roman prelates, if they submitted to the Pope; they also suggested that a considerable degree of autonomy would be granted to the episcopate, while the laity would no longer be allowed to participate in the administration of Church affairs.

The plan for " Unia " was discussed in great secrecy. Its promoters wanted to secure the signatures of all the bishops to the act of submission, in the hope that the rest of the clergy and the laity, seeing the entire episcopate had gone over to Rome, would be obliged to follow their example. As far as this part of the plan was concerned, the supporters of Unia were greatly mistaken, for they did not understand the mentality of the Eastern Christians. The desertion of the bishops could not frighten the laity into submission. On the contrary, it would only inflame them with renewed zeal for Orthodoxy.

The chief advocate of " Unia " was Bishop Ignatius Pociey. Before his ordination in the Orthodox Church he had passed through Calvinism and Romanism, and had made many contacts among the Latin clergy. His main concern was to win over the senior hierarch of the Orthodox Church in the Ukraine, Michael Ragosa, the Metropolitan of Kiev. The latter was a weak though pious man, who could not make up his mind whether or not to join the Uniats, and while he was still deliberating, rumours about his impending apostasy reached the Orthodox population.

At once Prince Constantine Ostrozhski [1] (d. 1608), the great Russian magnate, patron of learning and a staunch defender of the Eastern tradition, issued an eloquent epistle denouncing the secret negotiations conducted by the hierarchy. Three of the bishops, alarmed by this disclosure, drew back and declared their determination to remain Orthodox, but the rest decided to act quickly. Ipatius Pociey and another bishop, Cyril Terlecki, hastened to Rome and made their formal submission. Pope Clement VIII warmly welcomed the two prelates and a special medal was minted bearing the inscription " Ruthenis Receptis ". Meanwhile the Church Council was convoked in Brest Litovsk in 1596. The vast majority of clergy and laity were opposed to " Unia ", but most of the bishops favoured it. The Council was split, and each party excommunicated the other. The Orthodox were greatly assisted by the presence of two Greek bishops, Nichiphoros and Cyril Lukaris, who represented the Patriarchs of Constantinople and Alexandria.

King Sigismund Vasa III (d. 1632), who was an ardent Roman Catholic and pupil of the Jesuits, declared the Orthodox members of the Council to be rebels against Church and State. Bishop Nichiphoros was arrested and starved to death, whilst Cyril Lukaris, the future Patriarch of Constantinople, escaped the same fate only by precipitate flight. A regular persecution was launched; the Orthodox Churches were closed, the priests were arrested and the laity had to endure every form of humiliation and insult. In spite of all these measures, Orthodoxy survived, whilst the Uniat Church proved a failure.

---

[1] The first printed Bible in Slavonic was published by his private printing press. He founded also the first Orthodox College for higher education.

The Roman Catholics looked down on it as an inferior form of Christianity; the Orthodox treated it as an apostate body. The Uniat bishops were never admitted to the Senate, and those Russians and Lithuanians who wanted to get on in Polish society preferred to join the Latin Church and thus obtain full political rights, an honour which was never bestowed upon the Uniats.

" Unia " failed to establish a link between Eastern and Latin Christians. It did not bring reconciliation, which would have profited both sides, but instead the spirit of animosity was increased to such an extent that it provoked an outbreak of civil war in the Ukraine and White Russia. The negative results of this attempt at reunion were due to the mixed motives behind it. " Unia " was not the outcome of a desire for unity arising in the hearts of the divided Christians, but a cleverly conceived plan strongly coloured by political and selfish considerations, and for this reason it could not cure the sin of schism.

" Unia " opened a hard and protracted struggle between the Orthodox Christians and the Polish State. The Eastern Church survived in the Ukraine because spiritually it received powerful support from the lay brotherhoods, and because politically it was protected by the military force of freedom-loving Cossacks.

Deserted by the majority of their bishops, persecuted by the Government, the members of the Eastern Church found the best weapon of self-defence in lay brotherhoods, which sprang up in all parts of the country. The movement began in Lvov, the capital of Galicia, and from there it rapidly spread over the other centres of Eastern Orthodoxy, such as Kiev, Luck, Przemysl, Vilno, Minsk, Mogilev. The Patriarch Jeremiah, on his way to Moscow in 1588, stopped in Kiev and Galicia and granted special charters to these brotherhoods, authorising them to exercise control not only over their own members, but even over bishops and parochial clergy. One of the chief activities of these brotherhoods was the provision of schools, which they opened in all the great cities. As a result, a new type of better-trained leaders was secured. One of them, Mileti Smotritski, in 1610, published a book entitled *The Lamentations of the Eastern Church*, which described the miserable state of the Orthodox so eloquently that it stirred public opinion in Poland, where the question began to be raised whether the persecuting zeal of the Uniat bishops was not preparing the ground for rebellion in the Ukraine, instead of converting the Orthodox to Rome.

These warnings, however, were disregarded by the King and the leaders of Church and State. The policy of oppression was vigorously pursued, and the Orthodox Church suffered grievously. The most serious blow was the extinction of its episcopate. The Government firmly refused to grant the Orthodox permission to ordain bishops. Amidst these calamities a new power, the Cossacks, appeared on the scene, radically altering the situation and providing the Orthodox with a sturdy weapon of self-defence.

The southern steppes had been a no-man's land since the time of the Tartar invasion. The constant danger of sudden attack by the nomads made it too dangerous a place for a peaceful population to live in. But these steppes attracted dissatisfied and adventurous men who preferred the risks of war to serfdom and oppression. These freedom-loving men, known as Cossacks, formed a number of self-governing communities. Their main centres were situated along the lower reaches of the rivers Don and Dnieper. The Cossacks were ready to fight the Tartars, the Turks, the Moscow Tsardom or Poland; they owed allegiance to no one and were their own masters. There was nothing in their early history to suggest that they could ever become the champions of the Orthodox Church, but this was the rôle which they assumed in the seventeenth century. This transformation was effected by " Unia ". The majority of the Cossacks were of peasant origin, and they resented the power and privileges of the landlords. The introduction of " Unia " further increased this antagonism to the upper classes; for the rural population in the Ukraine, besides suffering economic oppression, became exposed in the seventeenth century to persecution which was provoked by its faithfulness to Eastern Orthodoxy.

The admixture of a religious element deeply stirred the Cossacks. Their struggle against the gentry acquired new significance. A class war was transformed into a holy crusade; and expeditions which aimed at plunder and robbery of the rich were interpreted as part of the fight in the defence of the true faith. The Cossacks possessed considerable military power, and, when the Orthodox realised that they could rely upon their

THE ORTHODOX IN POLAND AND LITHUANIA

support, they no longer felt helpless and abandoned by all. The new centre of resistance was fixed in the Theological Academy in Kiev, founded in 1615 by the generosity of a Russian woman named Elizabeth Gulevich. The school was situated sufficiently near the camps of the Cossacks to enable its professors and students to feel safe under their protection. The members of the college started an energetic campaign in the defence of their Church, and they were greatly assisted by the fact that, in 1620, Theophan, Patriarch of Jerusalem, on his way to Moscow, secretly ordained seven Orthodox bishops. Though the Polish authorities immediately issued an order for their arrest, this could not be executed, because the Cossacks took them under their protection.

Their new rôle as defenders of the hierarchy and patrons of theological learning greatly appealed to the Cossacks, and they began to exercise an increasingly strong pressure upon the Government of Poland. Many of the sons of the Cossacks enlisted as students of Divinity at the school, the very existence of which depended on the bravery and fighting skill of their fathers.[1]

The Academy reached the climax of its importance under Peter Mogila (1596–1647), the most remarkable among the Metropolitans of Kiev. The son of a Moldavian prince, he belonged to the highest aristocracy of the realm. Educated in Paris, he was at home in Latin culture, but, contrary to the general tendency of his time among the gentry, he remained devoutly Orthodox. He greatly surprised his friends when, at the age of thirty, he gave up his military career and took holy orders. He became at once the recognised leader of the persecuted Church. In 1632, King Sigismund Vasa, the ardent supporter of " Unia ", died. The sejm of the Polish and Lithuanian nobility elected as his successor his son Wladyslaw IV (1632–48), who, realising the dangers of an oppressive policy, granted several concessions to the Orthodox, of which the chief was the recognition of their right to have a Metropolitan in Kiev. Peter Mogila was immediately elected to that See, and, from 1633 till his death in 1647, he ably directed the life of the Orthodox Church. His episcopate forms a turning-point in the history of

---

[1] A picturesque description of the relation between the Academy and the Cossacks is given in the famous novel *Taras Bulba* by Gogol, available in an English translation.

Eastern Christianity, for he drastically altered the whole system of teaching in the Kiev Academy and, with it, the general trend of Eastern theology. His reform consisted in adopting for use by the Orthodox the programme of training devised by the Jesuits for their own Colleges. Even the language of instruction was changed to Latin, the students had to listen to Latin lectures, to read Latin books, to preach sermons in Latin. This was a striking departure from tradition, and only a man of Peter's energy and authority could have carried it through in face of determined opposition.

Peter Mogila was convinced that the Orthodox Church needed men of the same intellectual ability and learning as the Roman and the Protestant Churches had, and, because in the seventeenth century no one could be considered educated who was not able to read and write fluently in Latin, he forced the Orthodox to master the tongue which they associated with the enemies of their faith. He himself remained a supporter of the Eastern tradition, and the acknowledged purpose of his reforms was to arm his church against the assaults coming from the West; but the method he used created an entirely novel situation. Peter Mogila latinised the thought and worship of the Eastern Christians. The catechisms he composed repudiated the Roman claims, but in terms borrowed from the West; the Slavonic prayer books he revised were Orthodox indeed, but here and there the text included expressions and ideas hitherto unknown to Eastern Christians, but found in Roman Catholic manuals—such, for example, as the use by the priest of the personal pronoun in the formula of Absolution in Confession. Peter Mogila, realising some of the consequences of his innovations, tried to win over his critics, and he submitted his revised prayer books and catechisms to the judgment of the Council composed of clergy and laity held in Kiev in 1640. In 1643, another Council was held in Jassy in Moldavia, to which Greek and Russian theologians were invited. These gatherings gave their approval to Mogila's work, for there seemed to be no other way than that chosen by the Metropolitan for raising the standard of learning among the Orthodox.

Thus a new period in the history of the Eastern Church was inaugurated. The Orthodox were brought into the battlefield of Western ecclesiastical controversies, equipped with modern armour well-designed to resist Roman and Protestant attempts to convert them; yet, to some extent, they lost their identity—the very object for which they had been fighting.

This latinisation of Eastern theology, which was so ill-suited to its temper, lasted for more than two hundred years. Only in the middle of the nineteenth century did a movement for the return to its proper tradition set in, first in Russia; later, in the twentieth century, its influence became felt in the Orthodox countries of the Balkans. As far as the Ukraine was concerned, Peter Mogila's reforms marked the final breakdown of any hope of solving the conflict between the Eastern and Roman Catholic Christians under Polish rule by any means other than open contest. The Roman Church was not strong enough to annihilate the Orthodox, yet its members were not prepared to tolerate the co-existence of the Eastern Christians in their midst by granting to them the status of equality. Both sides began to arm for the bitter clash which occurred towards the end of Mogila's life.

A powerful rebellion of the Cossacks, supported by an uprising of the peasants, swept the whole Ukraine. Its leader, Hetman Bogdan Khmelnitski (d. 1657), having defeated the Polish army, (1648), forced King Jan Kasimir (1648–68) to make important concessions. The King promised to withdraw the Jews, the Jesuits and the Polish troops from the Cossacks' lands, granting wide autonomy to the Orthodox. The peace was, however, soon broken, and this time the Cossacks were defeated by the Poles. In despair, Bogdan appealed to Moscow for help. The National Assembly, after much hesitation, decided in 1653 to come to the rescue of the Orthodox in Ukraine, and, on January 8th, 1654, the " Rada ", the General Assembly of the Cossacks, recognised Tsar Alexis Romanov as their sovereign.

War between Poland and Russia flared up and lasted for thirteen years, neither side being able to defeat the other. The peace concluded in 1667 was a compromise. All the lands on the left bank of the Dnieper passed to Moscow, but the right bank remained in Polish hands, with the exception of Kiev, which was temporarily ceded to the Russians. The Cossacks were bitterly disappointed: they had not only failed to secure their autonomy, but they were even divided between Poland and Russia. Yet their failure was the cause of far-reaching changes in the destiny of their two neighbours: Poland was mortally wounded; and Russia, too, was profoundly affected, for her long isolation had been brought to an end. By incorporating people who had lived under Western influence for two centuries, she received a powerful current of new ideas. The stronghold of Orthodoxy, hitherto closely guarded against the outside world, was forced to open its gates. Its inhabitants, at last, painfully realised their inferiority in military and technical matters. The Moscow Government was obliged to plan a number of reforms, but these were so strongly resented that a serious split occurred inside the nation and the Church. This split is known under the name of The Great Schism.

CHAPTER XI

THE GREAT SCHISM IN THE RUSSIAN CHURCH

MICHAEL ROMANOV (1613–45), who had been elected by the largest and most representative National Assembly ever held in Moscow, at which seven hundred delegates were present, had the moral backing of the entire nation, and he needed it. The task of reconstruction was formidable: the country was ruined, its population scattered and depleted, and vast territories had been occupied by foreign enemies. The young Tsar relied upon the continued assistance of the National Assemblies, which were held at frequent intervals during his reign (1613–15, 1616–18, 1619, 1620–22, 1632–34, 1637, and 1642), but, unfortunately, he found few outstanding men to shape a new policy. The bulk of the Russians felt bewildered and so frightened by the horrors of " the time of troubles " that they merely wished to return to the old order at whatever price. This mentality affected all spheres of Russian life. For instance, the new dynasty was an elected one, but instead of recognising this fact, its representatives behaved as if they had been members of the old House of Rurik, and justified themselves on the ground that Ivan the Terrible, by marrying Anastasia Romanova, had incorporated them in his family.

Again, the National Assemblies were no longer mere consultative organs, as they had been in the sixteenth century—they held supreme authority over the life of the nation—but their leaders still talked as if they had no duty but that of offering advice.

As a result, many defects of the old order were reintroduced for no other reason than the desire to perpetuate the familiar pattern, and many mistakes were made, of which the most grievous was the failure to improve the lot of the peasants. In fact, this became worse, new and heavy obligations being imposed upon them.

The Church, also, was caught in this current of excessive conservatism, a misfortune due to the personality of the new Patriarch, Philaret Romanov (1619–33), the father of the Tsar Michael. He was one of the leading figures of the Moscow ruling class and, during Boris Godunov's reign, had been obliged to take monastic vows in order to save his life, for he was looked upon by the Tsar

as a possible rival. Captured by the Poles, Philaret was released
by them in 1619, and on his return to Moscow he was immediately
elected as Patriarch, the See having been kept vacant for him
since Germogen's death, in 1612. Philaret was a devout man
with a genuine love for beauty and dignity in worship. He
greatly improved Church discipline, which had become slack in
the years of anarchy, but his primary concern was not the Church,
but the State, and till his death he was the actual ruler of Russia.
The weak son was completely eclipsed by the domineering father.
Philaret even took the title of " The Great Lord ", hitherto
reserved for the Tsar. He sat on the throne beside his son, all
State papers bore their joint signature, and his Court differed but
little from the Imperial Court. Philaret's exceptional position
raised the office of Patriarch to a height never reached before, and
the sphere of Church influence was widely extended, but the
results, from a spiritual point of view, were negative. The
Church lost its identity; its chief hierarch spoke with a voice which
sounded like that of a secular ruler, and this happened at a time
when the Government was pursuing a policy of reaction, and when
the nation was in desperate need of guidance from an enlightened
and independent Christian opinion. The Russian leaders ob-
stinately looked backwards, with the result that the nation headed
straight towards another crisis provoked by the dispute concerning
the authenticity of Russian Orthodoxy.

The crisis came in the middle of the seventeenth century, during
the reign of Alexis Romanov (1645–76). He was only sixteen
years old when, on the death of his father, he was elected Tsar by
the National Assembly. Personally, he was a very attractive man,
warm-hearted, sensitive to beauty, free from malice and conceit,
and genuinely devout. He loved and understood the sacred
pattern of Russian daily life (" obriad ") and all the customs and
traditions which embodied the deeply Christian outlook of his
people. As a ruler, however, Alexis was disappointing, and his
short-comings were as typically Russian as his achievements. The
culture of Moscow was a product of the heart and of the imagination; it was deficient in discipline and in law. Alexis was,
accordingly, impulsive, often generous; yet he could also be
arbitrary and despotic. He was the very embodiment of paternal
autocracy. The head of an enormous Empire, he tried to rule
it as his own big family, scolding and praising State officials like
his children. His intentions were good, but the results were

unsatisfactory; the country was run inefficiently and most of its urgent problems were never properly solved. As a consequence of this muddle, the kindest of all the Russian Tsars had to suppress with much brutality and bloodshed a mighty uprising of the peasants; [1] the most devout of Russian Sovereigns caused the schism in the Church; and the man who was himself an accomplished representative of the art of ritual living prepared the way for its disintegration and collapse.

Yet nothing at first suggested the possibility of such a tragic turn of events. On the contrary, the beginning of Alexis's reign promised a revival on an unprecedented scale. The Tsar was born in 1629, and he belonged to a generation of exceptionally gifted men who at last supplied first-class leaders for both Church and State. Especially remarkable was the high quality displayed by the parochial clergy, a class which had rarely played a conspicuous part in the life of the nation. The Russian priests, being married men, up till this time had usually been handicapped by large families and limited incomes. They had had little training, and all their time and energy had been taken up with the conduct of services. But in the middle of the seventeenth century, simultaneously, in different parts of the country, a new type of priest appeared on the scene—men of strength and conviction, eloquent preachers, excellent organisers, who boldly attacked the prevalent evils and were not afraid to challenge the greed and injustice of the wealthy and powerful, and the laziness and superstition of the ignorant and poor. These zealots firmly believed in the reality of Russia's mission to reveal to the world the truth of Orthodoxy, but they were equally certain that only a morally purified and regenerate people could follow this high calling; and they proclaimed that the recent misfortunes were the result of slovenliness and vice, which had eaten deeply into all the strata of Russian society. Their sermons brought them up against strong opposition, but neither exile, nor imprisonment, nor the attacks of the mob could silence them, for they were not alone. Many Russians generously responded to their appeal for moral improvement, among them the Royal Chaplain, the Archpriest, Stefan Vonifatiev, one of the best men of his time. Through his influence, the young Tsar gave his whole-hearted approval to the movement started by the provincial clergy, and several of these priests, such as Ivan Neronov, Avvacum and others, were transferred to Moscow and

[1] The revolt led by a Cossack Stenka Razin (1670–71).

put in charge of the leading churches of the Capital. The country was stirred, and signs of a spiritual revival were visible everywhere. Plans for far-reaching reforms were discussed, and these were connected in people's minds with the impending election of a new patriarch. The Patriarch Joseph, an old man in poor health, died in April 1652, and the party of reformers hoped that the Archpriest, Stefan Vonifatiev, their beloved leader, would be invited to occupy this post. The Tsar, however, had set his heart on another candidate, Nikon, the Metropolitan of Novgorod, of whom Dean Stanley, one of the first Englishmen to try to fathom the unexplored depths of Russian Church History, gives the following description: " Nikon is unquestionably the greatest character in the annals of the Russian Hierarchy. . . . Throughout all the obscurity which hangs over him, there is yet discernible a genuine human character, combining with a wilful, barbaric obstinacy as of an overgrown spoiled child, the caustic humour and the indefatigable energy of a statesman of the extreme West." [1] To call Nikon the most outstanding of Russian hierarchs is an over-statement, but he was certainly one of the most tragic figures among them, for he inflicted a shattering blow upon the Church which he genuinely wanted to serve.

Nikon was born in 1605. He was the son of a poor peasant, and, like the majority of Russian leaders in the seventeenth century, he came from the region of Nizhni Novgorod. His childhood was unhappy, and he fled early from his home. He was very gifted, and the monks of a neighbouring monastery took an interest in him and taught him to read and write. At the age of twenty, Nikon was married and ordained. His fame as a priest spread rapidly. No one who ever met him could forget his striking figure. He was dark, tall and handsome; he had a magnificent voice, was deeply devout and, above all, he possessed an inexhaustible source of energy. He had also a gift for doing everything in the grand style and was endowed with original and exquisite artistic taste. Russia owes to Nikon's passion for building some of the best churches of the seventeenth century. [2] He was soon transferred to Moscow, where he suffered a grievous loss—all his three children died. He was very impressionable, and apt to act on impulse. He immediately resigned from his parish, and both he and his wife joined religious communities.

[1] A. P. Stanley, *History of the Eastern Church*, Everyman ed. 1927, p. 327.
[2] The famous monastery of New Jerusalem was one of the architectural gèms. It was blown up by the Germans during their retreat in 1942.

The Tsar Alexis first met Nikon in 1646, when the latter came to Moscow as Abbot of a small struggling community, lost in the tundras of the extreme north. Nikon at once produced such an impression upon the emotional and devout Sovereign that he was offered the charge of the Novospassky Monastery, the burial-place of the Romanov family. Alexis frequently visited the tombs of his parents, and his admiration for Nikon grew every day. He was particularly impressed by the Abbot's unfailing solicitude on behalf of poverty-stricken and unjustly-treated people. A constant stream of petitioners went to see Nikon, and he was always ready to bring to the Tsar's notice those cases which deserved attention. Alexis became convinced that no one in his realm had such a following as his friend, the monk.

In 1648, Nikon was elected to the Metropolitan See of Novgorod, where he distinguished himself by quelling a local revolt, and in 1652 he was offered the Patriarch's Throne. At first he refused, but reluctantly consented after the Tsar and the members of the Council had prostrated themselves before him, imploring him to accept their invitation. He exacted, however, from the leaders of Church and State a solemn promise " to keep unchanged the commandments of Christ's Holy Gospels and the Canons of the Holy Apostles and of the Holy Fathers, and to obey the Patriarch as their chief Pastor and supreme Father ". This unusual declaration indicated that he was aware of a coming storm and wanted to secure, beforehand, obedience to his orders. Nikon started his reforms in Lent 1653, by ordering that the ritual of the services, including the manner of making the sign of the Cross, should be changed and observed henceforth according to the Greek fashion. This injunction profoundly shocked the whole nation and provoked especially bitter indignation among the reforming priests.

The purpose of Nikon's innovations and the reason for the violent opposition to them have often been misinterpreted by historians. The whole incident has been represented as the Patriarch's attempt to improve various minor points in the ceremony of Orthodox worship and to correct the text of Service Books by comparing them with the Greek original. The refusal to accept the changes has been explained as an example of ignorance and narrow-mindedness among the clergy and laity, who suffered such confusion as to the essential and the non-essential in religion that they preferred to split the Church rather than sing Alleluia three times instead of twice, or make the sign of the Cross with three fingers instead of two. In reality, Nikon and his opponents were not quarrelling over nothing; they fought each other on a major issue, which was bound to have a profound effect on all Eastern Christians, and especially on the Russians. The question which divided them was whether the Church of Moscow had the right to act as the sole leader of Orthodoxy, or whether her rôle was to be only a partner, and even a junior partner, in the movement for the regeneration and liberation of the Christian East. It was the most urgent practical problem of that time. A quick decision was required from the leaders of the Russian Church and State, who were hard-pressed by the unbearable conditions which the Eastern Christians had to endure outside the Moscow Tsardom. In Turkey, for instance, the Orthodox Church became in the seventeenth century a helpless victim of the bitter strife between the conflicting interests of the great European powers, besides being exposed as before to the arbitrary rule of the hostile Mahometans.

France, being a champion of the Latin Church, began to use her political influence against the Orthodox, trying to bring about their submission to Rome; England and Holland, representing Reformed Christianity, urged the Eastern Christians in the opposite direction. The secular and ecclesiastical diplomats of the West did not scruple to bribe the Turkish officials in order to get rid of the Orthodox prelates who were unwilling to serve their purpose. Cyril Lukaris, the learned Patriarch of Constantinople, lost his life, in 1638, as a result of the intrigues of the Roman Catholics, and he was only one victim among many others.

In Poland and Hungary, the position of the Orthodox Church was in no way better. The Catholics and the Protestants, usually irreconcilably opposed to each other, were ready to forget their quarrels in order to launch a joint attack against the Christians of the East. In Transylvania, for instance, a law was passed (1571), according to which the adherents of the Roman, Calvinistic, Lutheran, and Unitarian [1] Confessions were treated as equals, but the members of the Eastern Orthodox Church were ostracised and deprived of the rights of citizenship.

In this time of universal distress, the Eastern Christians turned

---

[1] An extreme wing of the Calvinists which denies the doctrine of the Holy Trinity.

to Russia, the only independent Orthodox State. An increasing number of visitors came to Moscow from all parts of the Eastern Church. They asked alms for their poverty-stricken dioceses and also implored the Russians to rescue them from their oppressors. Their claim for help was based on the conviction that the Tsars, as the successors of the Byzantine Emperors, were the protectors of all Orthodox Christians. The hour struck when the belief in Moscow as the Third Rome had to be tested practically, and the Russian Government was determined to fulfil its obligations. This involved readiness to wage a war against Poland and Turkey, both powerful military States, for nothing short of open conflict with them could alleviate the plight of the Eastern Christians in those countries.

The essential condition for success in such intervention was close co-operation between the Russians who intended to help and the other Eastern Christians who asked for assistance. Their mutual trust, however, was seriously undermined by a number of misunderstandings created by the divergences in their Church customs. The more the people of Moscow mixed with their co-religionists from beyond the borders, the more suspicious they became concerning the purity of non-Russian Orthodoxy. The first thing which surprised the Russians was the lack of reverence among laity and clergy from abroad. According to Moscow standards, the latter displayed a shocking ignorance of the most elementary points of churchmanship. The Russians, who were great artists in the conduct of worship, had evolved an elaborate and beautiful rhythm for their Services, which was lovingly observed by clergy and people alike. The Services lasted for many hours, and every minute detail of ceremony was carefully noted. Other Christians, who lived in poverty and under oppression, had had, of course, no similar training, and their casual manners during service were deprecated by the Russians. This was, however, a minor point compared with the chief problem confronting both sides. There was a serious discrepancy in the texts of their respective Service Books and in the ritual these contained, which affected, for instance, such vital acts as the manner of making the sign of the Cross, or the wording of the Creed. The word for Orthodoxy, " Pravoslavie ", means in Slavonic " the right glorification ", and the Russians ascribed the utmost importance to the visible manifestations of their inward belief. The sign of the Cross was for them the confession of faith in the

Holy Trinity and in the Incarnation, conveyed, not by means of words, as in the Creed, but by means of a bodily action.[1] To the Russians, with their special aptitude for plastic art, movement of head or arm was as important a channel of expression as the spoken word. It was inevitable that the Russians should pay great attention to small differences in ritual, for every action had its symbolic significance and had the tradition of centuries behind it. If the Greek theologians of the fourth century were ready to be martyred for the sake of one vowel in a word of the Creed, so the Russians of the seventeenth century were ready to suffer for the proper manner of making the sign of the Cross.

The cause of these differences in ritual, discovered by the Russians in the seventeenth century, was their long separation, under the Tartar yoke, from the rest of Eastern Christendom. For whilst the Church of Byzantium had gradually altered liturgical customs, the Russians had preserved intact the ritual received by them at the time of their conversion in the tenth century. The idea of evolution was foreign to the minds of both Eastern and Western theologians in the seventeenth century. Therefore when any difference was discovered, it was interpreted as the failure of one of the Churches to preserve intact the Apostolic tradition. The Russians had no doubt that the Christians from abroad were the guilty party, and they had strong reasons for such a conclusion. The Muscovites possessed ample evidence that their rites and customs were those of their fathers and forefathers, but this could not be said about the rest of the Eastern Christians. The Orthodox in Turkey, for instance, were not allowed to have their own schools or printing press. If they wanted theological education they could obtain it only in the colleges of the Western Christians, and their tuition there had, as a rule, to be paid for by a renunciation of their own Church. The young men from the Balkans had to become Papists or Protestants, whilst learning abroad, but on their return home they rejoined their Mother Church and fought in its defence with the weapons borrowed from their heterodox teachers. The Russians argued that such a schooling, bought at the expense of apostasy, was bound to affect the purity of the faith of their unfortunate co-religionists. They were, therefore, not surprised that the devotion and worship

[1] This point can be illustrated by the present custom of saluting another person by means of a verbal welcome and by a handshake. These two acts complete and strengthen each other.

of those Christians showed grave defects, and they insisted that the Moscow standard was the only one which could be trusted.

This point of view was commonly accepted in Russia, and was particularly strongly upheld by the priest-reformers, who preached that Russian Orthodoxy had to be made so bright that the whole Universe might be illuminated thereby. This idea was, however, bitterly resented by the Greeks, who, though poor and oppressed, affirmed that they had introduced the Russians into the Orthodox Church and that therefore they were their teachers in all matters of faith and worship.

The material dependence of the Eastern Christians on alms received from Moscow made them for a long time reluctant to start an open controversy, but the tension was growing and the question, which of the Churches was the guardian of unpolluted Orthodoxy, required proper solution.

Nikon's first Pastoral Epistle caused widespread consternation because he, the Patriarch of Moscow, solemnly declared in it that the Greeks were right and the Russians wrong on all points in which they differed from one another. This pronouncement, made without any previous consultation with the leaders of the Church, and in open defiance of the opinion of the most devout Russian Christians, naturally provoked an outburst of indignation and was interpreted as the betrayal by the newly elected Patriarch of the sacred cause committed to his charge.

The motives which prompted Nikon's drastic decision were these: he was well aware that the Tsar's main concern was to smooth out the differences between Russian and other Eastern Christians, and to unite them in a common endeavour to restore the freedom of the Orthodox Church. He knew, also, that Alexis believed that his favourite—the Patriarch—was the only man who could find the way out of this deadlock, and he decided to prove to the Tsar that this confidence was deserved. Nikon possessed tremendous driving power; he was impulsive and quick. His spectacular elevation from the poverty and misery of his home-life to intimacy with the Tsar gave him a strong self-assurance. He had no means of influencing the Greeks, but he trusted his own authority over the Russians and therefore decided to force them, by a simple decree, to give away their claims to superiority and to submit to Greek customs.

The Patriarch's self-confidence blinded him to the rashness of his action, for he hurt the most sensitive spot in the nation's religious life. The bulk of the people had no courage to resist openly the pressure of his and the Tsar's authority, but this was not the attitude of the zealot priests and their lay supporters. They were daring enough to declare that in no circumstances would they give up their belief in the superiority of Moscow tradition over that of other branches of the Eastern Church. The effect of this declaration was shattering. That a group of parish priests should dare to disobey the highest representatives of the Orthodox Church and State could hardly have been imagined in Russia before. Nikon was staggered, and he committed his second blunder: he made an attempt to intimidate his opponents by persecution. They were arrested, ill-treated, unfrocked, and sent into exile. All these measures were useless. He had no knowledge of the men and women who withstood him. Avvacum, Longuin, Lazarus, Boiarynia Morozova and other leaders of the opposition were not made of the stuff that yields under pressure; they were not afraid of torture and exile; and persecution only inflamed their zeal and strengthened their conviction that Nikon was a traitor, a false shepherd, to be opposed to the end by all faithful Christians. For the next five years, Russia was the scene of an amazing contest between the all-powerful Patriarch and this handful of priests and laymen.

The Tsar Alexis kept himself in the background. He spent most of his time with his army in Poland, fighting on behalf of his oppressed fellow-believers, whilst Nikon assumed the supreme leadership both in Church and State. Like Philaret, he took the title of " The Great Lord ", and he acted as Regent in the absence of the Tsar. He was not a success in his double rôle. Enraged by the stubbornness of the opposition, realising that the nation's sympathy was on the side of the persecuted, he behaved as a dictator, offending the boiars, alienating the best of the members of the Church, and relying on the help of self-seeking and unscrupulous adventurers, such as the Metropolitan of Gaza, Paisius Ligaridis, who was notorious for his readiness to serve those who paid him most.

In 1657, Alexis returned to Moscow and found the capital seething with discontent against the Patriarch. The Tsar's unbounded admiration for his friend began to cool. The change in his Sovereign's attitude was a blow to Nikon's pride and, greatly annoyed, he made yet another cardinal mistake. On July 10, 1658, at the end of a service, he uttered public complaints against Alexis and announced his intention of vacating the Patriarchal Throne. He probably hoped that the Tsar, having heard the news, would rush to the church and publicly ask him to change his mind. But the Tsar only sent two boiars, assuring Nikon of his friendship. This mediation was rejected by the Patriarch, who retired to one of his monasteries. For eight years, Russia remained without an acting Patriarch. Nikon played for time, neither resigning nor consenting to resume his office. The Eastern Patriarchs were consulted, and several councils were held, but opinions differed, and till 1666 no formal decision was taken. In that year, a Council, momentous in the history of the Russian Church, was assembled in Moscow. It lasted two years and was the most tragic as well as the longest of all Russian Synods. It was presided over by two Eastern Patriarchs, Paisius of Alexandria and Macarius of Antioch; but the main figure at the Council was Paisius Ligaridis, who by that time had become Nikon's principal accuser (although the Patriarch had formerly been his most generous benefactor). The Council acted as a demolition squad, pulling down one after another all those hopes, beliefs, and ideals which had given such courage and driving power to the nation. During its dramatic sessions, the leaders of Church and State publicly renounced the vision of Moscow as the Third Rome, which the Russians had embraced since the fifteenth century.

The first act of the Council was a solemn condemnation of all those who adhered to the traditional order of the Russian Church. Avvacum and his supporters were excommunicated. Thus the split between those who accepted and those who rejected Nikon's reforms in worship was perpetuated, and the body of the so-called Old Believers, or Old Ritualists, was created, which till the present day has commanded the allegiance of several millions of Russian Christians.

The second act of the Council was to depose the author of the reforms. The Patriarch was unfrocked and imprisoned, the charge being his unlawful desertion of his See and disrespect shown to the Sovereign.

The third act was the refutation of the Council of 1551, the most revered of all Russian Synods.[1] Its members had explicitly declared that Moscow Orthodoxy was the pattern for the rest of the Eastern Church, and the Russian Bishops, in 1667, were obliged to renounce this claim. Hard pressed by the arguments of Paisius Ligaridis, they reluctantly signed the following

[1] v. p. 56.

statement: " We declare the Council of 1551 to be no Council at all and its decisions not binding, because the Metropolitan, Macari, and those with him acted and made their decisions in ignorance, without reason, and quite arbitrarily, for they had not consulted the Oecumenical Patriarch."

The Old Believers refused to accept the judgment of the Council; Nikon, too, loudly protested. He behaved with great dignity during the trying procedure; his erect, imposing figure gave the impression that he was the judge of his accusers. Nevertheless, he was condemned and spent many years in confinement. He died on August 17, 1681, having outlived Alexis and most of his foes. He was buried, not as a simple monk, but with all the honours that belong to a Patriarch, and with that title he has remained in the memory of the Russian people.

Such is the strange story of the peasant who, for five years ruled the Russian Church and State, who had so many outstanding gifts and yet so little wisdom in using them. He rent asunder the Church which he so deeply loved and prepared the collapse of the order which he represented so typically himself.

W. Palmer,[1] Nikon's biographer and admirer, saw in him a champion of Church independence against the encroachment of secular forces. Nikon took that line of defence when he was brought before the Council of 1666/7. The facts do not support this claim, however. He was the victim of confusion, in his own mind, between Church and State, and between his personal impulses and the responsibility of his high office. He was at his best when he took to the Tsar the complaints of the people, disregarding the cumbersome legal procedure; he was at his worst when he inflicted heavy penalties upon the protesting clergy without bringing them before the proper ecclesiastical court, or when he left his office because he was hurt by his friend, Alexis. The latter behaved in a similar manner. At the Council of 1666/7, the Tsar bitterly complained of Nikon, but the character of his incriminations was entirely personal.

Nikon's drama was the drama of Russian culture; his fall was the fall of the Moscow Tsardom. Therefore, before considering the next stage of Russian history, it is necessary to summarize the failures and the achievements of that culture which had grown up round the city of Moscow.

[1] Palmer, *The Patriarch and the Tsar* (6 vols.), London, 1871–76.

CHAPTER XII

THE FAILURES AND ACHIEVEMENTS OF
MOSCOW CULTURE

THE order which the Russians had built up after their liberation from the Tartars was severely shaken by the Great Schism, and the cause of this was Moscow's inability to meet the challenge of restored contact with the wider Christian world. The responsibility for this failure rested upon the Party of the Possessors, who, for a hundred and fifty years, controlled the political and spiritual life of the nation. Under their exclusive leadership the development of Moscow culture became one-sided; it reached a high level of perfection in some directions and was lamentably deficient in others. But the sense of self-sufficiency which was so strongly marked among the Possessors blinded them to their limitations and made them unwilling to co-operate with other nations. The Possessors' chief mistake was their complete trust in the power and stability of Paternal Autocracy. Under their inspiration the Moscow Tsardom produced a political order in which oriental despotism and a genuine family spirit were curiously blended. The Tsars of Moscow were not only called Fathers by their people; they were such in reality, and this in spite of their often arbitrary rule. They and their subjects had the same interests, mentality and language; they formed one closely-knit body, for they all belonged to the same Church, which made no distinction between rich and poor, powerful and weak, but treated all its members as brothers.

The Russians sincerely desired to shape their social and political order in accordance with the pattern of a Christian family, but the external circumstances of their life were most unfavourable to the success of their endeavour. They inhabited a land with exposed frontiers; they were constantly attacked by their hostile neighbours; they suffered all the disadvantages of an intemperate climate, immense distances and undeveloped industry. Faced with all these obstacles, the Party of the Possessors tried to solve the difficulties by curtailing individual freedom, and in order to compensate for this departure from brotherhood, they substituted the symbolism of the Christian family for the everyday application of this ideal.

The Russians, with their strong artistic bent, were too ready to forget that the profound experience of unity and freedom, during Church services and on other ceremonial occasions, could not redeem the serfdom of the peasants and the oppression prevalent in their political and social conditions. The lofty Christian ritual of their home life, the warmth and beauty of their worship, were not strong enough to stand the weight of inequality and economic exploitation. The whole edifice was bound to collapse in spite of the vigour and inspiration of those who had planned and built it, and this happened in the second part of the seventeenth century.

It was particularly tragic that, at that decisive hour in Russian history, the leadership in the Church should be in the hands of men who overstressed the importance of ritual. There was no more striking representative of this mentality than the Patriarch Nikon himself. He brought the tradition of Moscow piety to perfection. The churches he built, the vestments he wore, were the finest examples of the Russian idea of beauty; his magnificent voice easily filled the largest building in the realm; his massive figure towered above any congregation. He was charitable to the poor, genuine in his devotion to the Church and to Christ; and yet the same Nikon could be brutal and even cruel. He knew how to command but had no idea how to consult; he stood for obedience and disliked discussions; he was rigid to such a degree that any idea of compromise or of gradual growth was repugnant to him. He always wanted to do things in his own way, and therefore he was more destructive than constructive. His main weakness was that over-confidence which characterised the rest of the Party of Possessors. A considerable section of the Russians became so enthralled by the vision of their special calling that they lost touch with reality. Instead of serving and helping other Eastern Christians, they began to despise their brethren who groaned under the yoke of foreign domination. As a result, Russia was deprived of her position of leadership and had to undergo a long period of cultural enslavement to the West, which challenged the exclusiveness of her people and their feeling of superiority.

The collapse of Moscow culture, however, must not obscure the greatness of its achievements. The Russians had a firm grasp of some fundamental Christian values, and they knew how to apply them in practice. Their spiritual life was centred in the Holy Eucharist; belief in the Incarnation was the driving power behind their art, their thought and all their social activities. They were profoundly convinced that this world, notwithstanding its imperfection, was intended to become the glorious temple of the Holy Spirit, and that man was empowered by God to be the chief agent in the process of this transfiguration. Man was made of dust, infected by sin, and yet he was the bearer of the Divine Image. He was exalted above all other creatures and endowed with the gift of intimate communion with the Maker of the Universe. Wilful disobedience made man the victim of disintegration. His physical existence was threatened by the chaos and enmity prevailing on earth; his inner life was distorted by his passions, selfishness and fears; and yet man, through his love and free obedience to the Incarnate Lord, could revive the shining beauty of the Divine Image within himself and restore harmony and peace in the world around him.

This conviction was expressed by the Russians through the medium of two words, " Obraz " and " Obriad ". Their English equivalents, " image " and " rite ", only remotely explain the Russian content of these two fundamental ideas. " Obraza " (plural of " obraz "), or religious pictures, were, for the Russians, not merely paintings. They were dynamic manifestations of man's spiritual power to redeem creation through beauty and art. The colours and lines of the " obraza " were not meant to imitate nature; the artists aimed at demonstrating that men, animals and plants, and the whole cosmos could be rescued from their present state of degradation and restored to their proper " Image ". The " obraza " were pledges of the coming victory of a redeemed creation over the fallen one. The expression of the Saints in these pictures was severe and ascetic; their movements were restrained, but their robes were shining, and their faces turned towards the new and better world. Hope and joy were expressed in their eyes, and the contrast between the immobility of their bodies and the intense liveliness of their looks emphasises the complete control of spirit over matter achieved by the Saints. This victory had a cosmic significance, for in man and through man the whole Universe was restored to its proper purpose: the glorification of its Creator. In times of peace, and in moments of danger, at home or on a journey, in the happiest hour of his life, and at the point of death, a Russian wished to see an " obraz ", to touch and kiss it and be comforted by it. The importance attributed to ikons seems to be shocking to foreign observers of Russian life, but for the Russians the artistic perfection of an ikon was not only a reflection of the celestial glory—it was a concrete example of matter restored to its original harmony and beauty, and serving as a vehicle of the Spirit. The ikons were part of the transfigured cosmos and, therefore, they could uplift the spirit of man and assist human beings in their struggle against disunity, disease and death. The veneration of ikons was based on the same belief that underlies the Eucharistic doctrine: as the Bread and Wine become the bearers of a new spiritual power, brought into the world through the Incarnation, so ikons also manifest the close interdependence between matter and spirit and the reality of their redemption. A further illustration of the same idea is provided by " obriad " (ritual or rite). This word, in Russian, means the code of behaviour which, if followed by a Christian, secures to him control over his mind and body and gives him mastery over the physical world. This code included the proper form for the worship of God, the type of relations with other human beings, corresponding to the Christian revelation, and the right attitude to material things like dress, food and money. The way people greeted each other, or expressed their sorrow and joy, the various kinds of meals they ate at different seasons, the decoration of their houses, and the architecture of their churches—all these were used by the Russians as parts of their corporate efforts to transform this world into the temple of the Holy Spirit. The material and the spiritual were treated as two sides of the same reality, and for this reason the smallest details of daily life were charged with religious significance. The unity of Russia during the Moscow period was neither national nor political: it depended mainly on the knowledge of " obriad ", and the Russians have a special expression " Bytovoe Blagochestie "—which describes this highly developed art of ritual living.

The acceptance of the same pattern of life constituted a powerful link uniting all the Russian people. They felt that they were one big family because they all believed in the same truth and followed the same path. Some of them proceeded satisfactorily, others lagged behind, but they all moved in the same direction, not because they were constrained to do so, but because they all accepted the same definition of man's origin and nature, and this supplied Russian life with spontaneity, warmth and freedom, even in the absence of political and economic liberty. The Russian vocabulary powerfully confirms these ideas. The men and women who have achieved moral victory are called " prepodobnye ", which means the most like to the divine Prototype. Every kind of ugliness and distortion is branded by the word " bezobrazie ", which, literally translated, means that which is without image or form.

The great vision, which inspired the Russian people, of the coming transfiguration of all creation, was also reflected in the interior decoration of the churches built during that period. These were crowned with domed roofs which symbolised the heavenly sphere. The Lord and Creator of the world was represented in its midst, surrounded by the angelic hosts. Lower down, along the walls and pillars, the Saints were painted, gradually ascending to their heavenly glory, forming an unbroken chain between the Throne of the Maker and the crowd of worshippers. These were gathered together in order to be uplifted, purified and regenerated by the same grace of the Holy Spirit which had changed men and women of previous generations into victorious Saints of the Holy Church. The road to sanctification was open to everybody, and the precepts of the perfect life were summarised in words from the Sermon on the Mount, which were recited by the congregation at the celebration of the Eucharist. Western Christendom laid greater stress upon the Law, in the form of the Ten Commandments, or on obedience to the divinely appointed Head of the Church. The Russians drew their inspiration from the Beatitudes, the most challenging definition of the way leading to happiness and glory. A Russian could be a good man or a bad man; he could try to live according to the Sermon on the Mount or fail to do so; but none had any doubt that this was the final revelation of truth, the only pattern of life, designed by the holy, yet merciful God for the sinful yet glorious creature, man. The exterior of the church buildings provided still further illustration of the same teaching, for the brightly coloured cupolas symbolised the earth transformed and redeemed by Eucharistic prayer and made part of Christ's Kingdom.

On the flat plains, covered with a mantle of snow during the long winter, these churches with their red, blue and green walls and domes looked like fragments of another world which would one day appear in its full glory, not out of nothing, but from the material used for the present imperfect universe. Such was the message of the Russian Church expressed through its ikons, rites and architecture; and there are no better interpretations than these of the Russian people and of their religion.

The peculiar mixture of failure and achievement in this Moscow order can also be seen in the study of its outstanding representatives. Unfortunately there is a great scarcity of biographical material from the sixteenth and seventeenth centuries. One of the few exceptions is provided by Avvacum, the leader of the Church revival, and the staunch opponent of Nikon's reforms. He himself described his life of struggle and adventure. His striking personality is the very quintessence of Russian culture before its contact with the Christian West.

Avvacum was born in 1621, and, like the majority of Russian leaders of that century, he came from the province of Nizhni Novgorod. He was the son of a priest and was ordained at the age of twenty-two. He was endowed with exceptional powers; his bodily strength and endurance seemed to be inexhaustible. His zeal in proclaiming the truth of the Gospel knew no limits. He and his wife, a woman of courage and conviction, dedicated their entire lives to the defence of Moscow Orthodoxy, and no personal danger, not even the threat of death, could stop them from preaching its glory and power. Avvacum was an outstanding writer, the first to use colloquial Russian, and therefore the founder of Russian literature as distinct from works written in Church Slavonic. His autobiography, composed in 1673, is available in an English translation.[1] It is the best introduction to the Christian outlook, so deep yet so different from that of the West, which was shared by the Russian nation during the Moscow period of its history. The autobiography contains many episodes of absorbing psychological interest.

Particularly dramatic were the years spent by Avvacum in exile in Siberia. There is something Biblical about the intimacy of his relation to God, about his frank confession of his own strength and weakness, and about his description of the men and beasts that took part in his relentless struggle. The background of this story was provided, however, not by a small corner of the world called Palestine, but by the gigantic frozen spaces of Siberia, and

[1] *The Life of the Archpriest Avvakum, by himself*, translated and edited by Miss Jane Harrison, London, 1924.

Avvacum himself combined the ardour and faith of the Prophets of Israel with the shrewd, coarse yet profoundly humane outlook of a typical Russian peasant.

Ten long years Avvacum and his family spent in exile (1653–63). He was placed under the orders of Pashkov, the Governor of Eastern Siberia, who was one of those ruthless and daring pioneers who, at the head of small detachments of Cossacks and convicts, pushed the Russian frontiers farther east and added large slices of territory to the Moscow dominion. Pashkov was a law unto himself; he feared neither God nor man, and it was an entirely new experience for him to meet a person of Avvacum's spiritual stature. Though a defenceless convict, the zealous priest defied the formidable governor in the defence of justice and religion. Flogged many times, exposed without food or proper clothes to the deadly bite of Siberian frost, Avvacum, inflamed by his faith and supported by his iron constitution, survived all these trials. The climax of this fierce contest was reached when Pashkov, after four years of continuous journeying, having lost half of his small force from lack of food and exhaustion, ordered his son to lead an expedition against the Mongols. It was a risky adventure, and Pashkov consulted a wizard of a local tribe who went into trance in front of the camp and promised success to the Russians.

Avvacum was seized with disgust and indignation at the sight of triumphant paganism, and, forgetting in his own words the rebuke given to the sons of Zebedee by the Saviour for their desire to punish those who refused hospitality to them, he started to pray to God asking Him to strike the offenders. " I, accursed ", he writes, " cried with a great cry to the Lord, Hearken to me, God, hearken to me, King of Heaven, hearken to me, sweet Lord. Let not one of them return home, dig a grave for every one of them yonder, bring them to destruction, O Lord, so that the Devil's prophecy may not be fulfilled."

It was the uncompromising warrior against evil who prayed with these words, but Avvacum was also a loving and tender-hearted man, and he adds, " I was seized with pity for them, for my soul foresaw that they would perish ". Pashkov's son was a secret disciple of the fearless priest and much beloved by Avvacum. It tore the prophet's heart to think he had asked for the annihilation of his companions and friends. The expedition failed to return on the appointed day. Several more days passed and there was no news from the men. Pashkov, like the rest of the camp, knew about Avvacum's curse, and he decided to deal severely with the insubordinate priest. A torture chamber was prepared and a fire kindled. Avvacum's family was weeping, but he himself, with coarse humour, describes his state in the following words: " I was repeating prayers for my end. I knew what manner of cook he was and that few came out alive from his roasting." But Avvacum was not to die yet: at the moment when he was taken to be tortured, Pashkov's son, wounded, exhausted, but still alive, reached the camp—the only survivor of the ill-fated expedition. Pashkov's heart failed him; he had no courage to destroy the man who spoke to God and was heard by Him.

Soon after this episode, Pashkov received an order to return to Russia. He left behind a party of sick and wounded, unarmed and unprotected. Avvacum was put in charge of them. There was little hope that this body would ever reach their homeland safely; many months of travel across a hostile and unknown country separated them from the nearest Russian settlements. But to everybody's surprise, Avvacum brought all these people back. He ends his narrative with the following words: " For ten years, Pashkov has tormented me, or I him. I know not which. God will decide on the Day of Judgment." This final sentence is truly remarkable; it reveals how conscious he was of the power of Spirit. In this uneven battle, he was better-armed than his adversary: Pashkov had no other weapons but the knout, the hot iron and the bullet; he could torture and destroy Avvacum's body, but he had no power over his will. Avvacum, on the contrary, was able to inflict an agony of fear, hate and revenge upon his opponent, and he was able to bring over to his side Pashkov's wife and children, and to make the powerful governor utterly lonely even in his own household. Avvacum's faith helped him to triumph over the greatest sufferings, and that was why not he, but his gaoler, was the true victim, and Avvacum knew it in the depth of his heart.

His story is not complete without some mention of the part played by his wife. She shared all her husband's trials; and incredible as it may sound, she even maintained their family life amidst the privations of their Siberian exile. She bore children and brought them up. Some of them perished from cold and starvation, others survived and were a source of joy and consolation to their parents. The woman was equal to the man, sometimes even stronger than he. Avvacum relates that when, after ten years of wandering, he at last reached the Russian settlements and learned, to his distress, that many men of his party had either perished or yielded to pressure, his courage left him, and he began to contemplate a compromise with the Tsar. And here is his own story of his talk with his wife: " And seeing that I was troubled, my wife came to me and timidly and delicately said: ' How comes it, my lord, that you are troubled? ' and I acquainted her with all my thoughts. ' Wife, what must I do, am I to speak or to hold my peace? ' " On her answer depended everything. Avvacum, if he ceased to oppose, would be restored to freedom; instead of exile and tortures, he and his wife and children could enjoy a life of honour, prosperity and Court favours. But this Russian woman was made of the same stuff as her husband, and she said: " I and the children, we give you our blessing to continue the preaching of the word of God as heretofore. Christ is strong, and He will not abandon us." " And ", adds Avvacum, " I bowed to the earth before her and shook myself free from blindness." At that moment Avvacum set his foot on the road to martyrdom, sent there by his wife and children.

The uncompromising priest, after a short sojourn in Moscow, was again banished, this time to the North of Russia. He spent fifteen years in prison, but neither his body nor his spirit could be broken. Cut off from direct contact with his followers, he reverted to writing. More than fifty works, including his auto-biography, date from that period.

He ended his life as a martyr, being burnt alive in 1682, with three of his closest associates. The official act declared that they were condemned to death for " the great blasphemies which they uttered in regard to the Tsar and his household ".

Avvacum's autobiography and Russian art of the seventeenth century are two sides of the same picture. They bear witness to the same cardinal fact, the overwhelming reality of the spiritual world to the Russians of that period. When Avvacum was asked by his friend how he could survive his ten years of exile under Pashkov and come safely home, bringing with him his family, the priest answered: " Christ brought me through, and the all-pure Mother of God brought me through; I fear no man, only Christ do I fear."

These were not mere words; they were the foundation of his life and conduct; and the same can be said of all the best men and women of his generation. This explains why the ikons they painted and the churches they built expressed so convincingly their belief that the spirit is stronger than the flesh, that good is more powerful than evil.

Life was hard in Russia, men could be brutal and in manners coarse; but they were single-minded and they had a clear scale of values. It was not always possible for them to live up to it, but in defence of truth they were ready to perish, for they had no doubts as to the ultimate purpose of life. They possessed that certainty of knowledge which was lost by the next generation of Russian leaders.

CHAPTER XIII

PETER THE GREAT AND THE ABOLITION
OF THE PATRIARCHATE

THE reign of the Tsar Alexis Mikhailovich inaugurated a period of transition in the history of the Russian people. Their centuries-long isolation was brought to an end, and a flood of new ideas, customs and institutions began to sweep over their realm. These changes were especially noticeable in the Capital. On its outskirts a suburb sprang up, called " the German Borough ", which was inhabited exclusively by foreigners, mostly technicians, employed, in increasing numbers, by the Government. Western dress, furniture, books, and even the theatre, made their appearance in the stronghold of Eastern Orthodoxy. Russia after an interval of five centuries once more met Europe, and the absorption of Western civilisation proceeded with ever-increasing speed. This was particularly marked in the change of outlook among those leaders of Church and State who were well-disposed towards the West.

The older generation of Westernisers was represented by people like Boiarin Feodor Mikhailovich Rtishchev (1625–73), and his sister Anna. They were examples of the high achievements of Moscow culture. They were both patrons of learning, and brought many first-class scholars from Kiev to Moscow. They were equally interested in charitable works, and several homes for the orphaned and destitute were founded by them. They also granted freedom to all their serfs and servants. The most remarkable feature of Rtishchev's character, however, was his personal integrity. In spite of his wealth and important position in the Government, he was so profoundly humble that he was ready to ask pardon publicly of his subordinates if he inadvertently offended them, and his generosity was such that no one was allowed to leave his house without obtaining some help. Rtishchev and his sister were intellectually open-minded and eager to acquaint the Russians with the best achievements of Europe, but they had no desire to make their country part of the Western world. They were convinced of the unique truth of Eastern Orthodoxy and deeply attached to the rhythm and customs of Russia's traditional life.

This enlightened nationalism was shared by their friend, the learned monk Epiphanius Slovenetski (*d.* 1676), who came from the Ukraine and settled in Moscow. Epiphanius belonged to the old pre-Mogila school of Kiev theology. He was steeped in the teaching of the Fathers, knew Greek well, and was a true scholar. He was mistrustful, however, of the Latin tendencies brought into the life of the Orthodox Church by Peter Mogila. Epiphanius was a conservative, but not a reactionary; he hoped to see his Church strengthened, not through imitation of the West, but by the rediscovery of its own tradition, obscured by centuries of Mahometan oppression and by the decadence of learning which followed. The scholarly elder was of a retiring disposition, silent and humble, but in times of crisis he could speak out with courage and authority. He was one of the few men who were not afraid to do justice to the Patriarch Nikon, after the fall of the great prelate, and he did it in spite of the fact that he had never been one of his admirers.

The next stage in the evolution of Russian society in regard to the West was represented by men like Simeon Polotski (*d.* 1680), and Prince Basil Golitsyn (1643–1714). These leaders of Church and State, though still staunchly Orthodox, were already enthusiastic admirers of Europe which they knew chiefly through the channel of Polish culture. Simeon, like Epiphanius, was a monk from Kiev, but he was trained under Peter Mogila and represented the urbane type of prelate hitherto unknown in Moscow. He spoke fluent Latin, composed poetry and was an eloquent preacher; he was not a real scholar, but he had a large amount of miscellaneous information, and he impressed the Tsar and the Court so much that the education of Alexis's children was entrusted to him.

Prince Basil Golitsyn followed the same trend of thought. He was a Westernised Russian who preferred European dress, furniture and manners to his own. He was proud of his good Polish and Latin, and his house was a place of welcome to all foreign visitors in Moscow. During his ascendancy (1682–89) he introduced several improvements in administration—all of them copied from the West. In politics he maintained a close alliance with Poland, a policy started by his predecessor, Boiarin Afonasi Ordyn-Nashchokin (*d.* 1681), the most outstanding Russian Minister of Foreign Affairs in the seventeenth century.

Epiphanius and Simeon Polotski typify the two schools of new learning which came to Russia in the seventeenth century. One of them belonged entirely to the Eastern tradition, and held Byzantine scholarship as its ideal; the other, although also Orthodox, derived much from the outlook and spirit of the West, and chose Polish culture as its pattern. These two schools of thought came into open conflict, after the Tsar Alexis's death, on the question of the time of the consecration of the Eucharistic elements. Simeon and his eloquent disciple, Sylvester Medvedev (*d.* 1691), held the Western point of view, that the consecration takes place when the priest pronounces the words of institution, " Take, eat, this is my body . . ."; whilst their opponents, led by two learned brothers, Joanikius and Sophronius Lichudis, who came to Moscow from Greece, treated this opinion as erroneous and emphasised the invocation of the Holy Spirit as the climax in the act of consecration. For a long time neither of the parties could score a decisive success, but in 1690 a Council convoked in Moscow condemned the views of the leaders of the Westernising party, and censored several theological manuals published in Kiev, including some of Peter Mogila's revised prayer books.

This victory of the conservatives was of short duration, for far-reaching political changes soon made the Church entirely dependent on the State.

The story of these years of transition with their new problems, disappointments and bright hopes would be incomplete without mentioning a lonely enthusiast for Russo-Western co-operation, a Croat, a Roman Catholic priest, Iuri Krizhanich (1617–78). He was the first Slavophil, a man who ardently believed in the unity of all Slavonic nations, and who preached the ideas which caught the imagination of Russian leaders two hundred years later and which still remain a task to be achieved. Krizhanich was a man of great gifts, a first-class scholar and theologian, a linguist and a politician. He travelled all over the Near East, and was well-acquainted with the position of the Slavs in Austria and under the Turks. He came to Russia in order to impress upon her people the urgency of their mission to unite and liberate their brethren abroad, oppressed by Germans and Mahometans. He arrived in Moscow in 1659 and, in his own words, he came there " not as a wanderer who has no home, but as a man who returns to his own nation, to his own sovereign, to a land where his service could be useful and his labours appreciated ".

The Russians met him as they met other visitors from the West, with their characteristic mixture of warm hospitality and suspicion. For some unknown reason, Krizhanich was soon exiled to Siberia, but his banishment was not altogether a misfortune. His freedom was not restricted, he enjoyed a liberal Government stipend and he could give all his time to the development of his favourite idea—that the Russians and the Western and Southern Slavs needed each other; that their joint efforts could restore the unity of the Church and bring peace and stability to Europe, for he insisted that the Slavonic nations were not aggressors, like the Germans and Turks, and had no desire to dominate their neighbours. His historical, theological, and philological works contain much fresh and stimulating material. Unfortunately only a small portion of them has so far been published, but, with the passage of time, the importance of his thought becomes more and more apparent. In 1677, Krizhanich returned to Moscow, revealed the fact that he was a Roman Catholic priest, and was allowed to return to Europe. Nothing is known about him for certain after he had left Russia.

Such were some of the leading men engaged in the search for the best means of collaboration with Europe. Different schemes were discussed, and a more conservative and more radical policy was advocated, when suddenly a storm descended upon the country and swept Russia into the turmoil of a mighty cultural revolution.

This was caused by the accession to the throne of Peter the Great (1682–1725), the youngest son of Alexis Mikhailovich! Alexis had married twice, and had nine children by his first wife, Miloslavskaia, and a son, Peter, by his second wife, Naryshkina. His eldest son, Theodor Alexeevich (1676–82), was only fourteen years old when he inherited his father's throne. He was an attractive young man, benevolent and inspired by good intentions. With the aid of a group of gifted assistants, he began to introduce various well-planned reforms, but he died prematurely in the middle of these improvements. His death created a complicated question of succession. His brother next in age, Ivan, was a slow-witted youth, unfit to govern; on the contrary, his half-brother, Peter, showed signs of great mental and physical vigour and, though only ten years old, seemed best suited to be Tsar of Russia. The families of Alexis's first and second wives, the Miloslavskis and the Naryshkins, entered into a fierce contest for power. At first the Naryshkins were victorious, and they proclaimed Peter as the sole ruler. But they were quickly defeated, and the Miloslavskis, supported by the " streltsy "—the permanent militia—established by the Tsar Alexis, carried through a Court revolution. A crowd of drunken soldiers invaded the Kremlin, and several members of the Naryshkin family were murdered by the mob before the eyes of the terrified boy, Peter, who, however, showed remarkable self-control on this occasion. As a result of this uprising, Ivan and Peter were proclaimed joint rulers, whilst Sophia, the twenty-five-year-old daughter of Alexis, became Regent. She was an intelligent and masterful woman, who with great skill and determination conducted the affairs of the State, till she was forced to give up her power after a short but fierce struggle with her half-brother Peter, which flared up when he reached the age of seventeen.

Until 1689, the young Tsar had lived in banishment from the Court, constantly fearing for his life, for Sophia and her family regarded the boy as their chief enemy. His education had been neglected and no attempt had been made to introduce him to the sacred pattern of daily life which was the pride and joy of the Tsars and people of Moscow. Peter grew up as a wild plant having no roots in the traditions of Russian culture. On the contrary, he associated it with all that he hated and feared in his childhood and adolescence.

By nature, Peter was a man of action, possessed of inexhaustible energy; he was skilled in every kind of handwork, and one of the greatest joys of his life was toiling on the wharf and building ships, for such work satisfied his desire to be always busy in mind and body. Uninfluenced by the elaborate ceremonies of Church and Court, or the discipline of the classroom, his character was formed amidst affrays, which he himself staged with skill and enthusiasm between two companies of village boys. Peter hated any kind of restriction imposed upon him from outside; he obeyed only the dictates of his impulsive personality. Yet he was not a common tyrant, for he wanted to serve his country, and he spared no sacrifice or effort in order to attain this goal.

His aim was to make Russia a great military power, properly industrialised, efficiently organised—in short, to give his realm an important place among the nations of Europe. He had an unbounded admiration for the West; everything that attracted him he found there; everything that he disliked he associated with Moscow culture. He was not only a reformer, he was also an avenger, and his enemy was the old Russia, the representatives of which had made him suffer helpless rage and paralysing fright in his early years.

Peter the Great was a colossal figure. Single-handed, he changed the course of Russia's history. He defeated all his foreign enemies, crushed opposition at home and re-opened sea communication with Europe, a task which the nation had not been able to accomplish since the Tartar invasion. A mighty stream of new life poured into the country. The creative genius of the people was awakened through contact with the wider world. Russian literature and science came into existence; secular painting, harmonised music, the ballet and the theatre reached a high level of perfection.

But these remarkable achievements were bought at an extravagantly high price. The growth of cultural collaboration between Russia and the West had already started in the seventeenth century, and Peter was not its first promoter. His rôle was to transform the pace of gradual evolution into the torrential movement of a violent revolution. By doing this, he destroyed the unity of the Russian people. He introduced a system of government alien to the spirit of the nation; he created a deep gulf between the upper classes and the rest of the population; he enslaved the peasants and paralysed the Church. He deeply wounded the most sensitive and sacred feelings of the people and inadvertently gave away the Russian Throne to greedy and unscrupulous foreign adventurers.

This destructive aspect of Peter's reforms was yet another act of the drama that opened with the victory of the Possessors in the time of Ivan the Terrible, and reached its climax during the Great Schism. The paternal autocracy to which the party entrusted the preservation of Moscow Orthodoxy became the instrument of its humiliation and degradation. The concentration, which they advocated, of all authority in the hands of the monarch, made it possible for Peter to smash into pieces that very order which the Tsars were supposed to protect against all external and internal enemies.

The Russians regarded their Sovereigns as the divinely-appointed fathers of the nation. The Tsars did not wear military dress, like the Kings of the West, but sacred vestments symbolising their moral and religious authority.   In spite of the failures and sins of individuals, the Moscow rulers aspired to the ideals of holiness, humility and forgiveness.   Peter profaned this Russian conception of a Christian Sovereign.   To the horror and consternation of his people, the Tsar, whose predecessors had not even carried arms, acted as a public executioner, beheading rebellious soldiers with his own hands in the streets of Moscow. Instead of being a dignified and solemn figure, an example of piety to all his people, Peter behaved like a Westerner of low birth, drinking, smoking, and swearing in the company of Dutch and German sailors and mercenaries.   The Russians, who treated foreigners as people who had no idea of the conduct proper to a Christian, were humiliated by the sight of their own Tsar imitating the manners of uncouth ruffians.

Peter was aware of the universal disapproval with which the nation regarded his reforms and his personal life.   He knew also that the centre of opposition was the Church, for it was the traditional channel for the expression of the moral opinion of the nation, which even Ivan the Terrible had been obliged to respect.   He could not, however, tolerate any interference with his supreme power, and he decided to reduce the Church to that state of subordination to the secular rulers which, as he learned during his visit abroad, existed in Protestant countries.

The Russian Church as a corporate body has never tried to assume political authority.   The Patriarch, as the spokesman of the Church, had, however, the right, sanctioned by age-long tradition, to appeal to the Christian conscience of the Sovereign and, in the name of love and forgiveness, to ask him to change his decisions.   This right, called in Russian " Pechalovanie ", represented the universally-held belief that the Tsars, more than anybody else, were in need of divine grace, guidance and forgiveness, for they carried upon their shoulders the heavy burden of power which corrupts and saps the integrity even of the best Christians.   The Church therefore offered special prayers for the Tsar, and the hierarchy felt a particular responsibility for directing and advising the Sovereign.

Peter was not afraid of the Church as a political opponent, but he could not accept its right to judge his actions morally. When, in 1698, the Patriarch appeared at the head of a procession and asked the Tsar to show mercy on the guilty Streltsy, Peter sharply rebuked him and declared that the bishops had no right to speak on matters of military discipline. This meant the end of the old Moscow order, for Peter drew a line of demarcation between secular and ecclesiastical spheres, which existed in the West, but which hitherto had been unknown to the Russian people. By this act, he ceased to be the Tsar of Russia, becoming instead an Absolute Monarch with the Western title of " The Emperor ".

Peter achieved this radical change at the price of destroying the harmony which had previously existed in Russia between the Church and the Tsardom. He deprived the Church of its freedom and imposed a compulsory silence upon its members. For two hundred years, it had to remain in captivity to the Empire. It was a formidable task to reduce the Church to this subordination, and it could never have been achieved in normal circumstances. But Peter struck his fatal blow at a time when the Church was grievously weakened by the Schism; when many of its devout members had been obliged to form their own schismatic bodies of Old Believers; and when those who remained in the Patriarchal Church felt bewildered and disunited among themselves. Furthermore the bishops were just then exposed to the rivalry growing between the Moscow clergy and those who came from Kiev. Peter acted with caution and skill. He was aware of the people's profound devotion to the Church, and therefore, instead of directly assaulting it, he used other methods to secure its gradual enslavement. His first step towards the establishment of State control, as represented by the absolute will of the monarch, was to postpone the election of a new Patriarch after the death of Adrian in 1700.

Instead of convoking the usual council, he nominated Stefan Iavorski (d. 1722), Metropolitan of Riazan, as guardian of the vacant throne. For twenty years the Church leaders were kept in a state of suspense, awaiting the Emperor's orders to meet for the election, but this order never came. Meanwhile, Peter did not waste his time but arranged that new bishops should be appointed from the ranks of those who were obedient to his will. His favourite was Bishop Theophan Prokopovich (1681-1738), an able but ambitious and unscrupulous man, who was ready to sell the freedom of the Church for Court favours. It was he who drafted a new constitution for the Church, published in 1721 under the title of " the Ecclesiastical Regulation ". This document completely altered the status of the Church and created a situation which had no parallel in the experience of Eastern Christianity.

The Ecclesiastical Regulation was an odd piece of legislation composed in the style of a controversial pamphlet. In it, Peter and Theophan sharply attacked the Orthodox hierarchy, criticised various customs and traditions, and, at the end, declared that the office of Patriarch should be abolished, for many Russians thought, erroneously, that the Patriarch was almost as important as the Emperor himself, whilst the latter, with his absolute power over all his subjects, was not to be compared with anyone else. Peter therefore decreed that the Patriarchate should be replaced by a collegiate body called " The Holy Governing Synod ". The constitution and the functioning of this organ had no precedents in the history of the Eastern Church. Peter copied it from the German Ecclesiastical Synods. He was a great admirer of Luther and praised him highly, because he had helped to bring the Church under secular control.

The governing Synod was composed of bishops and other ecclesiastical dignitaries, not elected by the Church but chosen by the Emperor. They all had to take a special oath and declare : " I acknowledge the Monarch of all-Russia, our Gracious Lord, to be the final Judge of this College ". To make the new organ entirely dependent on his will, Peter appointed a secular official, called the Procurator of the Synod, to supervise all its proceedings. The Procurator, who represented the " watchful eye " of the Emperor himself, was not a member of the College, but nothing could be discussed or enacted without his approval. The Procurator acted as a most efficient brake on every movement of the Church hierarchy. If one adds to this control the Emperor's right to dismiss any member of the Synod and replace him by another candidate of his own choice, the helplessness of the Synod becomes apparent. Peter gave the Church no chance of discussing the proposed reforms in ecclesiastical administration. He knew too well that the reaction would be negative. Instead of convoking a Council, he dispatched special emissaries to individual bishops, asking them to sign the " Regulation ", and if they refused he threatened them with banishment. The frightened and demoralised bishops, one after another, gave their unwilling approval, expecting that so grotesque a caricature of ecclesi-

astical government would disappear with the death of the
monarch.   But they hoped in vain: of all Peter's hastily invented
institutions, the Synod lasted longest; it remained in action until
the very end of the Empire created by Peter on the ruins of the
Moscow Tsardom.

CHAPTER XIV

THE CHURCH UNDER THE ST. PETERSBURG EMPIRE

THE new Empire and its Capital were foreign plants in Russian soil. Peter rightly felt that Moscow, the true heart of the nation, could never serve as a centre for his bureaucratic and militaristic State, for Moscow was too deply rooted in the Byzantine tradition of Russian culture. St. Petersburg represented the Western secularised stage of the country's development, and accordingly the Court and the Government were transferred to the city bearing a foreign name, inhabited by strangers, and situated on the very fringe of the great Russian plain.

The Emperor, in his desire to break irrevocably with the past, went so far as to sacrifice even his own son, who was strangled because of his opposition to the reforms (1718). The father and Sovereign, having committed this crime, made a decree that authorised the Russian Emperors to leave the throne to anyone they chose. He himself failed to make use of this right, for he died suddenly, in 1725, and had no time to appoint his successor. For the rest of the century, the Russian throne became a playground for intriguing courtiers, foreign diplomats and officers of the Guards stationed in the Capital.

The Emperors and Empresses of the eighteenth century, who followed each other in quick succession, were mostly Germans by birth. They appeared strange, shadowy figures to the nation. Dressed in pompous French costumes or Prussian uniforms, often speaking only broken Russian, having the mentality and horizon of the petty princelings of the small German States, they were in most cases the pathetic victims of their abysmal ignorance, moral corruption and complete isolation from the rest of the country. They led an artificial existence in an artificial city, created by the dynamic will of Peter the Great. They and the society which surrounded them had no personality, no style of their own; they were crude imitations of the West, always trying to reproduce the last word in European fashion and manners.

Among these monarchs of fortune, the most attractive person

was one of Peter's daughters—Elizabeth (1741–61), but she completed the disservice to the nation begun by her father. Peter destroyed the lawful succession to the Russian throne; Elizabeth handed it over to a German youth, a Duke of Holstein also called Peter. He was a degenerate, with a passionate love for military uniforms, parade grounds and the whole spirit of the Prussian army. He could not imagine anything more inspiring than the atmosphere of a German barracks.

Elizabeth's nephew ruled over Russia, under the name of Peter III, for less than two years (1761–62), but his peculiar psychology was inherited by his son Paul I (1796–1801), and by both of his grandsons, Alexander I (1801–25) and Nicholas I (1825–55). It meant that the Russian Empire for nearly a century was governed by men whose outlook on life, habits and interests stood in sharp contrast to the sacred and cherished traditions of the Russian people, and whose idea of order and discipline was essentially German.

During the short reign of Peter III, a most important event in the evolution of Russian social order took place. The Emperor, in 1762, released the gentry from their obligation to serve the State; but, at the same time, the peasants were forced to continue to supply the landowners with free labour. Peter's decree meant a complete breakdown of the moral foundation on which the social life of the nation was built. Previously the lot of the peasant serfs was hard, but, though they could never be reconciled to the loss of their freedom, their heavy sacrifice, nevertheless, was to some extent balanced by the compulsory service to the nation which was extracted from the landed classes. Their male representatives had to enlist either in the army or in the civil administration and had to remain at the disposal of the Government during their whole life. The Emperor's decree demoralised the nation; it increased the resentment of the peasants, and at the same time it turned the upper classes into idlers, who benefited by the labours of others without rendering any service to the country themselves. The spread of extreme revolutionary opinions both among the gentry and the intelligentsia in the nineteenth century was the reaction of their most conscientious representatives to this injustice.

Peter III was murdered by conspirators, who proclaimed as his successor his young widow—a German princess, Catherine II (1762–96). Under her rule, Russia's army and fleet won many spectacular victories, the Court and aristocracy enjoyed the luxury and refinement of Western civilisation, but the common people suffered more than ever before.   In protest the peasants staged one of their most impressive revolts, by which, under the leadership of a Cossack Pugachev [1] (1773–75), they almost succeeded in overthrowing the rule of the foreign Empire.

Catherine saw herself as the benevolent ruler of a barbaric people whose main purpose in life should be to surround the great Northern Empress with splendour surpassing even that of the kings of France.   During her reign St. Petersburg blossomed out in all its extravagant beauty.   It was a typical example of a parasite plant inimical to native growths, and responding with admiration to all that came from abroad.   Catherine was fortunate in the service of several outstanding Russians, like Generals Suvorov (d. 1798) and Potemkin (d. 1791), the poet G. R. Derzhavin (1743–1816), writers such as D. I. Fonvisin (1745–92), Nikolai Novikov (1744–1818), Princess Ekaterina Dashkova (1743–1810) and others.   All these men and women lived in two different worlds; their roots were still in the old Moscow culture, but their upbringing, their habits and their important positions forced them to accept the artificial atmosphere of the St. Petersburg Court.

Two events of first-class importance marked Catherine's reign as far as foreign politics were concerned.   The first was the incorporation of the Crimea in the Empire in 1783.   This was the last stronghold of the Tartars, from which they still carried out their assaults on the Russian settlements.   This conquest made possible the colonisation of the rich southern provinces and secured an outlet to the Black Sea.

The second event was the partition of Poland in 1795.   It was a fatal blunder, for which the Russians had to pay a heavy price.   The neighbouring Slavonic State was divided into three parts: the old Russian territories, like Galicia, inhabited by Eastern Christians, were handed over by Catherine to Austria, whilst the purely Polish territories were incorporated in Russia. The rest was taken by Prussia.   This partition brought into the Empire a compact body of people who had no desire to be its partners; it opened the doors of Russia to a large Jewish population, and finally it placed the country among the aggressors, thereby compromising its traditional rôle as friend and protector

[1] See Pushkin's *The Captain's Daughter*.

of the Slavonic peoples suffering under the Mahometan and German yokes.

There is no better example of how alien the rulers of the St. Petersburg State were to the true interests and aspirations of the Russian people than the dismemberment of Poland, committed by Catherine and perpetuated by her successors.

The whirlwind of new ideas which blew into Russia from the West in the eighteenth century also affected the Church. The St. Petersburg Empire created a period of changes and tensions and unsettled conditions in the history of Russian Christianity. Peter the Great, in his revolt against the old Moscow tradition, had promoted to the leading ecclesiastical posts men trained in the Ukraine. They impressed him with their Western learning, their greater readiness to submit to secular control, and their opposition to Moscow exclusiveness, against which Peter fought so tenaciously all his life. These Ukrainian prelates displayed two distinct tendencies. Some of them were particularly antagonistic to Rome, and strove against the Latin Christians with weapons borrowed from the Protestants; the others were opposed to the Reformed Churches, and made use of the Roman Catholic arguments against the Calvinists and the Lutherans.

The most prominent representative of the anti-Latin school of thought was the learned bishop Theophan Prokopovich (1681–1736). Bishop Stefan Iavorski (d. 1722), who was appointed first President of the Synod, had an opposite leaning, and the two men had little to say in favour of each other. The Moscow clergy disliked all the newcomers, and regarded with equal distrust the Ukrainian theologians whether critical of Rome or hostile to Protestantism. They themselves had, however, few men of learning, and therefore were obliged to submit, at least for the time being, to the bishops trained in Kiev. The latter brought with them a type of scholarship which suffered from several defects. It followed too slavishly Western trends of thought and was too much involved in Western controversies. The theological seminaries which were opened in Russia in the course of the eighteenth century were all staffed with pupils of the Kiev Academy, and a new generation of clergy was brought up on text-books written in Latin and impregnated with a queer mixture of Protestant and Roman theology. The Orthodox point of view was represented in this literature as something

negative, neither Roman nor Protestant, occupying a neutral
position between these two extremes. This type of training did
great harm to the work of the Russian Church, for it made
the clergy a body apart, equally alien to the upper classes and
to the bulk of the people. Secular education in Russia, designed
for the gentry, imitated that of contemporary France or Germany,
whereas the masses of the people clung stubbornly to their traditional Moscow culture. But the outlook of the clergy was formed
in schools which were neither modern Western nor Russian. They
taught the decadent scholasticism of the Counter-Reformation,
brought into Poland by the Jesuits in the seventeenth century and
borrowed from them by Peter Mogila. The sermons the clergy
were trained to preach, the books they wrote, created little
response in any section of Russian society. They appeared life-
less and quaint to the upper classes, and foreign and artificial
to the peasants. It is typical that the very word for scholasticism
in the Russian language (" skholastika ") denotes something dry,
useless, having no connection with real life.

The eighteenth century ended with the tragic figure of Paul I,
who inherited the insanity of his father Peter III and, like him,
perished at the hands of Court conspirators.

The nineteenth century opened a new page in the history of
the Empire. The dynasty was at last stabilised, a fusion of
Russian and Western cultures seemed to have been achieved,
and Russia took a prominent place in the life of the Western
nations. But the impression of power produced by the Empire
was an illusion; deep-rooted contradictions sapped its vitality,
and the State founded by Peter failed to become the home of
the Russian people. A great opportunity for reconciliation with
the nation presented itself, but was not taken, at the time of
Napoleon's invasion in 1812. Napoleon attacked Russia in the
hope of splitting the country into two hostile camps. He was
aware of the gulf that separated the foreign-educated gentry
from the masses groaning under the yoke of serfdom. The
reaction of the people to the invasion was not what the enemy
expected. With spontaneous unanimity the Russians rose against
the intruders and drove them away. Napoleon's defeat was to
a large extent due to the resolute though unorganised guerilla
resistance of the peasants. They fought not only against the
invader, but also for their own freedom, hoping to secure release
from their bondage by their voluntary and heroic contribution

to the defence of their country. The victorious Russian army reached Paris, and, when it returned home, the eyes of everyone were fixed on the young and refined monarch—Alexander I (1801–25), whose will was supreme both in Russia and over Europe. The peasants expected from him a grant of land and their freedom; the liberal and enlightened minority of educated people dreamt of political reform and a constitution. But they were all disappointed, for Alexander failed to act at this important moment of Russian history. Charming in manner, highly cultured, he was yet inwardly divided; brought up in the sentimental atmosphere of the eighteenth century, he liked to make discourses on the brotherhood of man and to praise noble and lofty sentiments, but underneath this liberal decorum he was the same petty tyrant and narrow Prussian disciplinarian as Peter III and Paul I had been before him. Alexander was as much a foreigner in Russia as his father and grandfather, but they at least admired Prussia. Alexander admired nobody but himself. He completely failed to understand the aspiration of the Russian peasants and antagonised them by introducing agricultural settlements with Prussian drill and barracks regulations. Liberal circles in Russia were equally deceived by him; he promised much but gave nothing.

Russia was stirred, her hopes were raised high, but Alexander's inability to meet his people's desires sealed the Empire's destiny. He was unwilling to make it a paternal autocracy based on the support of liberated peasants, and he also refused to move along the lines of liberal reforms advocated by the Westernised upper classes. When the news of his mysterious death in remote Taganrog in 1825 reached the capital, a group of officers of the Royal Guard staged an unsuccessful revolt, the so-called Decembrist uprising, demanding the grant of a constitution. They were quickly suppressed by Alexander's brother and successor, Nicholas I (1825–55), who was the very personification of reaction. He was a man with a high sense of duty but was handicapped by a lack of sympathy with the nation which he had to rule. Like his grandfather, father and brother, he was at home only on the parade-ground, where he could admire the Prussian drill of his soldiers. He feared the discontented peasants and he mistrusted the educated classes; he was equally opposed to liberal ideas and to Russian nationalism. He governed his immense Empire with the help of a vast body of ill-paid officials, packed in the gloomy rooms of State buildings in remote and foreign Petersburg. With the obstinacy of a born autocrat, he suppressed freedom of thought and speech in his own country and tried to check by force of arms all liberal and national movements in Europe. He died defeated and disheartened by the Crimean war, which proved that his home and foreign policy was a complete fiasco.

His son, Alexander II (1855–81), introduced many reforms, the most important among them being the liberation of the serfs, in 1861. The changes, however, came too late to save the Empire, for they were not radical enough to be acceptable either to the peasants or to the educated classes. The rift between the bureaucracy of St. Petersburg and the rest of the country was rapidly widening, and Alexander was murdered by the group of extremists who, in their passion to imitate Europe, could not be satisfied with anything less than a republic with a radical social programme. The last stage of the Empire's decay was reached during the reigns of Alexander III (1881–94) and Nicholas II (1894–1917). In order to galvanise the dying body, a policy of aggressive nationalism, foreign to Russian tradition, was sponsored by St. Petersburg. Racial and religious minorities were victimised, and a pseudo-Russian style was encouraged in education, in art, and in political and religious life. During this last period the leaders of the Empire made persistent attempts to secure the support of the Church and to use its authority for the consolidation of the already tottering State. These efforts failed in their object. Only a free Church could achieve the spiritual revival of the Russian people, but its liberation from the bondage imposed upon it by Peter the Great had never been granted. Till its last breath, the Empire of St. Petersburg clung to its policy of suppressing the true voice of the Russian Church.

Externally, there were few outstanding events in the ecclesiastical history of Russia under the Empire. It followed obediently the course indicated by the Rulers. Under Catherine II, who shared the outlook of the French Encyclopedists and treated religion as a survival of barbarism, the Church had to pass through a process of purging which was hardly less than persecution. The Empress appointed, as Procurators of the Synod, men who openly professed atheism; monasteries and convents were closed; ecclesiastical property was confiscated, and the bishops who dared to protest were dismissed and ill-treated. One of them, Arseni, Metropolitan of Rostov, who had the courage to make a stand against the Empress, was even starved to death, in 1772, after a long and painful imprisonment.

During the reign of Alexander I, the Church had to endure the rule of Prince Alexander Golitsyn (1773-1844), who, according to the fashion of the time, exchanged his rationalism for pietism, which he tried to impose upon the Russian hierarchy. With the accession of Nicholas I, the Synod was handed over to Count Protasov, an officer in the Hussars and an upholder of discipline and subordination. A more liberal atmosphere was introduced into the administration of the Church during the reign of Alexander II, but this freedom was suppressed by the all-powerful Procurator Pobedonostsev (1827-1907), the advocate of extreme reaction. The attitude of the hierarchs to all these changes in the Government policy in regard to the Church appears at first sight to have been passive. With few exceptions, they all seemed to accept State control and to be reconciled to existing conditions. This impression, however, is misleading. Throughout the period of the Empire, the Russian hierarchy remained opposed to the Synod, and the desire for the restoration of Church freedom never died. Even such an over-cautious prelate as Philaret, the famous Metropolitan of Moscow (1782-1867), who was one of the most conforming bishops of the nineteenth century, never missed an opportunity of expressing his hope that the Church would one day be released from its bondage. Its members, however, were not revolutionaries, they had no intention of obtaining by force the rights arbitrarily taken away from them. They were law-abiding citizens, who hoped that the Government itself would some day recognise the injury to the national life caused by the enslavement of Christian opinion. Of the two partners, the one who lost more was not the Church, but the Empire, for, by refusing to Christians freedom of speech and action, the rulers of Russia deprived themselves of the benefit of friendly but independent criticism. They became morally isolated from the best elements of the nation, and they created around themselves that vacuum which caused the inglorious collapse of the whole State edifice in 1917.

The Empire of St. Petersburg vanished, but the Church survived the disaster and displayed an astonishing vitality during the years of storm and persecution.   In order to understand the source of its strength, one needs to study the inner spiritual life of Orthodoxy during those two hundred years when immobility and silence were imposed upon it by the State.

CHAPTER XV

SAINTS, MISSIONARIES AND PROPHETS

THE Great Schism and the centuries-long submission to the State that followed it weakened the grip of the Possessors on the Russian Church. Though their characteristic outlook survived, it ceased to predominate. The most significant consequence of the Possessors' defeat was the revival of the Non-Possessors' tradition, which quietly reappeared among the members of the Russian Church, bringing with it a renewal of missionary zeal, of healing and prophetic gifts, and providing the country with some remarkable examples of holiness and moral perfection.

This quickened spiritual life first showed itself in the religious communities, which were deeply stirred and purified by the repressive measures of Peter the Great and the persecution of Catherine II. The closing down of many monasteries and the confiscation of their lands drove some of the best monks into the wild forests of the north; others fled over the border and settled down on Mount Athos—the traditional stronghold of Eastern monasticism—or in the neighbouring Orthodox Rumania.

One of these monks, Paisi Velichkovski (1722–94), inaugurated a spiritual revival which raised the religious life of Russia to new heights comparable to those attained at the time of St. Sergius of Radonezh in the fourteenth century. Paisi was steeped in the teaching of the ancient Fathers and ascetics, and he had an outstanding gift for sharing his experience and knowledge with others. He was elected Abbot of the monastery of Niamets in Moldavia, where he gathered round him more than five hundred monks. Many of his disciples became great experts in the art of spiritual direction. These elders ("Startsy" in Russian) were men distinguished by their understanding of the most intricate problems of human life, and by their power to help others along the road of perfection. Many of them returned to Russia after the death of their teacher, and spread far and wide the best tradition of Orthodox monasticism, which had been obscured since the time of the Schism.

One of Paisi's great achievements was his translation of the ascetic writings from Greek into Slavonic. He introduced the

Russians to the spiritual wealth of Philokalia (" Dobrotolúbie "),
a collection of short extracts from the works of the Fathers,
dealing principally with self-examination, prayer and mystical
communion with God.

Two of Paisi's disciples, Theodor (*d.* 1817) and Kleopa
(*d.* 1822), formed a link between him and the most famous
centre of " Starchestvo " or spiritual direction in the nineteenth
and twentieth centuries—the " Optina Pustyn ". This monastery became famous throughout Russia for its succession of
inspired " elders ": Leonid (1768–1841), Makari [1] (1788–1860),
Amvrosi (1812–91), Iosif (*d.* 1911), Nektari (*d.* 1928), Anatoli
(*d.* 1922), were the best known among them. These wise teachers
of Christianity attracted a ceaseless stream of visitors from all
corners of the land. Men, women, old and young, rich and
poor, went to see them to ask their help, and no one was ever
rejected or refused assistance. These " Startsy " were concerned
not only with the spiritual problems of their visitors; they
were ready to discuss ordinary practical questions. A pilgrim
coming to consult a " Starets " would make confession of his
sins, but he would also quite naturally ask advice about selling
a cow or a house or about the marriage of his son or daughter.

The spirit of humility, of warm affection and genuine concern
for every human being, so markedly displayed by the " Startsy "
of the nineteenth century, was similar to that shown by St.
Nil of Sorsk (*d.* 1508) and other representatives of the Non-
Possessors. It was the same tradition, driven underground during the predominance of the Possessors' party, but never wholly
absent from the life of the Russian Church.

Not all the Startsy were monks, though the majority of them
were men and women who had embraced the religious life; but
some of them were married priests, others were lay people.
Such, for instance, was the famous elder, Feodor Kusmich, who
died in 1864 in Tomsk in Siberia. He was believed by many
to be the Emperor Alexander I, who, under that name, spent
the last years of his life in prayer and repentance.[2] This striking
theory has been accepted as plausible by several Russian historians
who have tried to solve the mystery which surrounded the life
and death of a homeless beggar, visited several times by con-
fidential envoys from the Imperial Court. Dostoevsky, who

[1] His letters are available in English: *Russian Letters of Direction,* selected and
translated by Julia de Beausobre, 1944.
[2] See Jarintzeff, *Russia, the Country of Extremes,* pp. 133–152.

stayed in Optina Pustyn in 1879, gives a vivid description of a
Russian Starets in *The Brothers Karamazov*, though Father
Zosima is not an actual portrait of any of the holy elders seen
by Dostoevsky himself. In Zosima, the great novelist combined
certain features he admired in the Optina monks with traits
belonging to an earlier representative of the same tradition, St.
Tikhon of Zadonsk (1724–83). The son of a poverty-stricken
Church reader, St. Tikhon was trained in one of the newly
founded seminaries, the Latin schooling in which presented such
a hard ordeal to the sons of Russian clerics in the eighteenth
century. Endowed with a lively mind, he progressed rapidly,
and in 1763 he became Bishop of Voronezh. He soon retired,
however (in 1767), and the remaining sixteen years of his life
were spent in seclusion in a monastery in Zadonsk. This with-
drawal from the world did not mean the inward severing of
connection with suffering mankind. On the contrary, St.
Tikhon gave himself whole-heartedly to the service of others.
In spite of poor health, he never slept for more than four or five
hours; the rest of his time was devoted to prayer and to helping
those who sought his advice. He maintained a large correspondence and, though he hardly ever left his bare cell, he was
always ready to receive visitors. He was the author of several
books on the spiritual life. He was a gifted writer, deeply
attached to his own Church, but friendly to the Christian West,
and he freely incorporated in his writings those elements of its
teaching which he found congenial to Eastern Orthodoxy.

The best known of all these holy teachers of modern Russia
was Seraphim of Sarov (1759–1833).[1] The son of a merchant,
he embraced the Religious life at the age of eighteen, and passed
through all the most difficult stages of purification and regeneration known to Eastern ascetic tradition. After seventeen years
of seclusion, silence and prayer, he opened the doors of his cell
(in 1825) to all those who wanted his help. An unending flow
of pilgrims began to move to the monastery of Sarov, lost in the
midst of the wild forests of the Tambov province. There were
days when between four and five thousand people knocked at his
door.

St. Seraphim was always dressed in white, and radiant joy
emanated from the Elder, whose bent body bore the traces of
long and hard struggle now brought to a victorious end. St.

[1] *St. Seraphim of Sarov*, trans. by A. F. Dobbie Bateman, London, 1936 and
The Flame in the Snow by de Beausobre, London, 1945.

Seraphim possessed the gift of healing; the innermost secrets of his visitors and of their future were opened to him, and nature responded to his prayers. He was a living example of the Kingdom of God manifested on earth through the perfect and loving obedience of a man to the Will of his Creator. In the midst of industrial revolution, scientific progress, and patronising indifference to Christianity among the upper classes, St. Seraphim shone as a chosen vessel of the Holy Spirit, comparable to the great saints and miracle-workers of ancient days. He proved that the Church does not grow old, and that the grace of God is equally effectual in all ages and in all places.

The same spirit of intimate and joyful communion with the Holy Trinity and full trust in God's healing and redeeming power was made manifest by Father John of Kronstad (d. 1908). Born in 1829 in the province of Archangel, he spent most of his long life as a parish priest in Kronstad, the naval base of the capital. He was able to touch the most hardened souls and reveal God even to men and women who deliberately closed their hearts and minds to divine influence. The number of people who wanted to confess their sins and to communicate at the services conducted by him was so large that he had to revive the ancient custom of public confession. He also possessed the gift of healing, and many thousands of people were cured by the aid of his prayers. His outlook on life, his vision of God, his deep knowledge of the unity of all human beings find expression in his diary, which, under the title *My Life in Christ*, has become a religious classic among Russian Christians.[1]

Father John of Kronstad and St. Seraphim of Sarov were great beacons whose light spread all over the country. They represented the spiritual rejuvenation experienced by Russia in the nineteenth century, for they were surrounded by other men and women who were blessed by a similar outpouring of the Holy Spirit. Only a few names can be mentioned here, such as Bishop Ignati Brianchaninov (1807–67), Bishop Theophan the Recluse (1815–94) (both remarkable for their writings on asceticism as well as for their integrity and wisdom), St. Ioasai the Bishop of Belgorod (d. 1754), Innokenti, Bishop of Penza (d. 1813), Antoni, Bishop of Voronezh (d. 1846), and monks and nuns such as Vassian and Parpheni of Kiev, Philaret, Abbot

---

[1] An English translation of *My Life in Christ* was published by E. Goulaeff, 1897.

of Glinsk (*d.* 1841), Vasilisk the Recluse, who lived in Siberia (*d.* 1823), and Anastasia, Abbess of the Pokrovski Convent in Kiev (*d.* 1900).

The Russian Church in the same period also had a revival of missionary zeal, and produced several outstanding preachers of the Gospel to the heathen. The Russians inherited from the Byzantine Church a keen desire to proclaim the Good News to those who had not yet heard it. From the dawn of their history they had sent out missionaries who worked among the Finnish and Mongolian tribes inhabiting the northern and eastern parts of the country. The best known among them was St. Stefan, Bishop of Perm (*d.* 1396), who displayed characteristically Russian concern for the preservation of the national identity of the newly-converted people. He was the missionary to the tribe of Zyriane, and he not only translated the Scriptures and the most important portions of the prayer books into their language, but even invented a special alphabet for them, composed of the signs he borrowed from their carvings and embroideries. He was convinced, as his contemporary biographer wrote, that every nation had to praise God in its own tongue in accordance with the peculiar gifts received from the Creator.

The missionaries in the nineteenth century were inspired by the same spirit that animated St. Stefan. They were all great linguists, who first mastered the languages of the Siberian and North American tribes, and, when this was accomplished, went to preach Christianity to those people. Such was the priest Makari Glukharev (1782-1847), who dedicated his life to the conversion of the peoples inhabiting Eastern Siberia. Another missionary priest was Ivan Veniaminov (1797-1879), the apostle of Alaska. After the death of his wife in 1839, he was ordained bishop of Kamchatka and the Kurelian and Aleutian Islands. His diocese included some of the most inhospitable parts of the world, and he was constantly obliged to risk his life in perilous journeys from one island to another, converting, baptising and instructing his growing flock, whose language and mentality he knew better than anyone else. His labours were crowned with God's blessing; the Church he founded became a living branch of Eastern Orthodoxy. Bishop Innokenti was a man of no influence at home, but his missionary zeal so much impressed the nation that he was elected in 1868 to the highest position in his Church, the Metropolitan See of Moscow.

Another famous missionary, in this case to the Mahometans, was a layman, Professor Nikolai Ilminski (d. 1891), who translated the Holy Scriptures into the colloquial language of the Tartars, Chuvash, Kirgiz, Kalmyk and other tribes inhabiting Eastern Russia and Western Siberia, and completely reorganised the methods of evangelisation among them. The Theological Academy of Kazan, where he taught, became a centre for missionary training.

Bishop Nikolai of Japan (1836–1912) was yet another outstanding Russian missionary. He went to Japan in 1860 as a chaplain to the Russian Consulate, and he spent at first four years in quiet study and prayer. His first convert was a Japanese called Sawabe, who had violently attacked Nikolai, accusing him of political conspiracy. In 1879, Nikolai was consecrated as the first Orthodox Bishop of Japan. .At his death in 1912 his Church numbered 30,000 members, and had reached the status of a self-supporting and self-governing body, with clergy recruited exclusively from among the Japanese.[1]

The life of the Russian Church in the nineteenth century was full of strange contradictions. Externally it was lamentably crippled by the deadly grip of the Empire, which imposed an artificial immobility upon Christian thought and action. But inwardly it was free and experienced an outpouring of the Holy Spirit greater than ever in its history. Officially, the Church was identified with the policy of Chauvinism pursued in imitation of Germany by the St. Petersburg bureaucracy, but the missionaries of the same Church taught the newly converted to love their own language and culture. Bishop Nikolai, for instance, deeply impressed his flock when, during the Russo-Japanese War (1904–5), he publicly offered prayers for the army of the nation of his adoption, which was fighting against his homeland.

The Church during the same period continued to preach the ideal of the Christian family, with its unity in freedom, as the sole pattern for the social life of a Christian State, yet it remained loyal to the Emperors who were hostile to freedom and tried hard to suppress the deeply rooted Russian habit of self-government and local initiative.

Finally, though Russian Christians continued to believe in

[1] For further information about his missionary activity see S. Bolshakoff, *The Missionary Work of the Russian Church*, 1943.

their special mission, and were certain that their Church had a message for the whole world, they witnessed the mass desertion from their ranks of the Westernised upper classes, who regarded their own Christian tradition as suitable only for an uncouth and primitive people. All these contradictions pressed heavily upon the thoughtful members of the Church, who tried to solve this puzzle and wanted to discern the future development of their nation.

The leading figure among them was Alexei Khomiakov (1804–60), one of the founders of the Slavophil movement. He belonged to the old aristocracy and was brought up, as were other young men of his generation and class, in the spirit of Western civilisation. He could speak and write in French, German and English with the same ease as in his own language. He knew Europe from the inside, but he was equally at home in Russia, which was the exception rather than the rule in Russian society in the first part of the nineteenth century. Through his mother's influence Alexei Khomiakov was deeply rooted in Eastern Orthodoxy, and he became its eloquent spokesman, able to explain the ancient tradition of his Church in terms familiar to modern Europe. In the middle of the nineteenth century, when belief in progress, science and individualism was universal, he had the foresight and courage to preach the approaching doom of an order based on the self-reliance of man and over-confident trust in the power of human reason. He boldly proclaimed that Russian Christianity, with its emphasis on the interdependence of all human beings and with its belief in Sobornost (unity in freedom), contained an important corrective for Western individualism, and that the Orthodox Church presented a better balanced and sounder interpretation of Christian truth than did either Romanism or Protestantism. Khomiakov's ideas interested only a small group of people who called themselves Slavophils; the majority of the educated classes were blinded by their admiration of Western civilisation and dismissed his teaching as the words of an eccentric. But he was not forgotten. In the second half of the nineteenth century many of his prophetic utterances were reaffirmed by the greatest of all Russian writers, Feodor Dostoevsky (1821–81), and by Dostoevsky's friend and disciple, the philosopher, Vladimir Soloviev [1] (1853–1900), whilst behind these two men stood

[1] The teaching of these three men is discussed in *Three Russian Prophets*, by N. Zernov, S.C.M. Press, 1944.

one of the most original and challenging of all Russian thinkers, Nikolai Feodorov (1828–1903), the man who drew some of the most daring conclusions from the mystery of the Incarnation ever made by any Christian theologian.

The message of all these writers was their conviction that the Russian people would be called to take a decisive part in the coming crisis of Western civilisation and that they would reveal to the world the true interpretation of Christianity. This meant that they supported the traditional belief of the Russians that their country was the third and last Rome and was to be the main scene of the coming clash between Christian and non-Christian forces. The teachers of the nineteenth century had moved, however, a long distance from the position occupied in the sixteenth century by the leaders of the Moscow Tsardom. They were aware that the Russian Church had first to be purged by tribulation and that only then could it fulfil its mission. They believed, also, that, not in proud isolation, but in humble service to the rest of Christendom, would its members be able to make a proper use of those hidden treasures which were entrusted by the Holy Ghost to the guardianship of the Russian nation. They were particularly distressed by the humiliating sub-mission of the hierarchy to the Germanised bureaucracy of the Empire, by the slavish imitation of the West on the part of the Russian intelligentsia, and by the ease with which individual Russians denied and sneered at the high calling to which their nation was summoned. Yet this apostasy, unfaithfulness and sloth were not able to destroy their prophetic belief in Russia's great future, and they were confirmed in this conviction by the examples of humility, forgiveness and holiness so often shown by peasant members of their Church. There, in the unknown depths of Russian life, these teachers discovered pearls of such complete devotion to Christ, of such intimate communion with the Holy Spirit,[1] of such a truly œcumenical vision of the Church, that they were sure that, in God's scheme for the redemption of the world, a special share was assigned to Russian Christians.

These thinkers had no doubt that Europe was heading straight towards one of its greatest crises. They described it as the con-test between those who believe in the self-sufficiency of man and those who profess the sovereignty of God as revealed by Jesus Christ. They saw clearly that behind the political, social and

[1] See *The Way of a Pilgrim*, translated by R. French, London, 1931.

economic conflict of their time loomed a much more tragic religious crisis, concealed from the sight of the common man, and yet exercising a decisive influence upon his thought and conduct. They described the choice which had to be made by civilised nations as a choice between the tyrannic, self-deified, totalitarian State and the challenging freedom of a Christian community. They knew well that the majority of men were afraid of the responsibilities of such freedom and were primarily concerned with security and material comfort. They realised that most people wanted to evade fellowship with the Holy Spirit and shrank from the overwhelming task of the transfiguration of the earth, assigned to the Church by God.

These Russian prophets were, therefore, prepared to see victorious those leaders who would promise bread and a life of ease at the price of apostasy from Christ; they were sure that they were living on the eve of one of the fiercest religious conflicts ever known in human history. They expected the clash to take place at the beginning of the twentieth century, and it actually occurred in 1917, when the Empire of St. Petersburg collapsed and the control of Russia fell into the hands of Lenin and his followers.

CHAPTER XVI

THE COLLAPSE OF THE EMPIRE, AND THE RESTORATION OF THE PATRIARCHATE

THE end of the Monarchy in Russia in 1917 and its replacement by the dictatorship of a party which represented the extreme form of Western Socialism caused consternation in the rest of the world. Suddenly, Russia appeared no longer as a devout Christian country, but as a militant godless State, fiercely opposed to any form of religion. This transformation created the impression that the Russians had probably never been earnest Christians, or, at any rate, that there was something fundamentally wrong with their Church if they could so quickly and absolutely reject its authority and teaching. The highly-coloured stories of its corruption and of the reactionary policy pursued by its leaders were accepted everywhere, for they seemed to provide an explanation of the unexpected change in the attitude of Russia to Christianity. The picture of a superstitious and subservient Church was so deeply imprinted upon the minds of Westerners that hardly anybody questioned its accuracy or asked to hear facts confirming it. Yet it is a caricature of the true condition of the Russian Church on the eve of the Revolution. It is vital that this wrong impression should be obliterated, for unless there is knowledge of the real situation, it will be impossible to understand the cause of that momentous struggle between Christians and atheists in which Russia has taken such a leading part.

The twentieth century found the Russian Church in a state of expectancy and awareness that far-reaching changes were at hand. During the nineteenth century outstanding men, such as Dostoevsky, Leontiev,[1] Soloviev and the Elders of Optina Pustyn sensed the approach of a crisis; but the majority of Church members took the established order for granted and believed that it would last for years to come. Externally, at that time, the Russian Church gave the impression of power and stability. Divided into 65 dioceses, having 130 bishops, 50,960 priests, 15,210 deacons, 20,000 monks, and 60,000 nuns living in 1026 Religious Houses, it numbered about 100,000,000 members, and

[1] See N. Berdyaev, *Leontiev*, London, 1940.

was the largest national Church in the world. But its inner condition caused grave concern in many ways. The chief evil from which it suffered was the compulsory silence imposed upon it by the bureaucratic control of the Empire. Apparently, the Church enjoyed a privileged position. The Emperors professed to be staunch defenders of Orthodoxy and, until 1905, any attempt to proselytise among its members was punishable by law. On all official occasions, lip-service was paid to the alliance between the Empire and the Church; but in reality the St. Petersburg Government knew well that the Church as the free voice of Christian people was opposed to its system of bureaucratic control. For this reason, special care was taken not to allow the Church to voice her true opinion: all books on religion were scrupulously censored, even sermons had to be approved by State officials in order to ensure that they contained nothing critical of the established order. No Councils had been held for two hundred years, and both dioceses and parishes had been deprived of every vestige of their previous self-government.

This state of utter powerlessness, to which Church administration was reduced, was emphasised by the iron rule of the Procurator, Constantine Pobedonostsev (1828–1907). The notorious advocate of a policy of chauvinism and reaction, he kept the episcopate in complete submission during his long tenure of office (1880–1905), constantly transferring bishops from one See to another—a practice forbidden by Canon Law, and thus depriving them of contact with their large flocks. He spared no effort to convince the country that the clergy, enforcedly silent, were behind his oppressive policy, and it was only after his fall, in 1905, that the falsehood of his claims was revealed.

That the Church, thus paralysed, should not properly fulfil its teaching mission was inevitable. The educated classes were indifferent and even hostile to the Christian faith; the masses were constantly attacked by the sectarians, who made a considerable number of converts, for, though their presentation of Christianity was deformed either by excessive mysticism or by rationalism, their independence attracted the devout.[1]

The status of the clergy was also unsatisfactory. They formed

[1] Russian sects are divided into two main groups: the first consists of the Baptists, Adventists and other types of Western Protestants; the second and largest represents various ramifications of the Old Believers movement. About three millions belong to the first, and about ten millions to the second group.

a class by themselves. Trained in fifty-nine seminaries and four theological academies, they were brought up in an atmosphere still reminiscent of the decadent Western scholasticism introduced into the Russian theological schools in the eighteenth century. The seminaries were not rooted in the life and tradition of Eastern Orthodoxy; they were yet another example of foreign influence thwarting the life of the Church. Many of their pupils left the schools, poisoned by hostility against religion, with the result that some of the most ardent revolutionaries came from the ranks of the seminarists. The life of a parish priest, from a worldly point of view, was unattractive. The clergy had large families and insufficient stipends, chiefly drawn from voluntary contributions in money and kind supplied by their parishioners and supplemented by the produce of small holdings which they usually had to work with their own hands. Sometimes, they had to give as much as half of their time to labour which was physically exhausting and poorly rewarded financially. The majority of the clergy received no salary either from the State or from the Church, and their income seldom surpassed a sum equivalent to fifty pounds a year. This meant that by their social status they were nearer to the peasant community than to the professional classes. During the time of serfdom, it was only on rare occasions that a village priest would be invited to the squire's house. This low social standing of the parochial clergy (one of the chief differences between Russia and the West) is often overlooked by foreign observers who write and speak about the Russian Church.

The poverty of the clergy forced them to send all their sons to Seminaries, where they received free tuition; the consequence was that these schools contained many pupils who had no vocation for the priesthood, and only a proportion of them were ordained. There were, however, periods in the nineteenth century when the Government, disregarding the true interests of the Church, required ordination of all those who had enjoyed free education in seminaries, and, as a result, the Church had to accept pastors who had no call to this work.

The chief defect of the clergy was their lack of authority: they were helpless against the petty officials who filled the diocesan offices and who were responsible to no one but the lay Procurator; they were also at the mercy of the local police, were looked down upon by the intelligentsia, and not much respected by the peasants on whose liberality they depended for their very existence.

The position of the bishops was not much better. They were chiefly recruited from the clergy class—there were only two or three examples in the nineteenth century of men belonging to the upper classes being consecrated, and this was considered to be socially degrading for them (another contrast between Russia and the West). The bishops were unmarried, mostly monks, sometimes widowed priests; and they were few in number. They were often men of intelligence, devotion and learning; but they never met at Conferences or Councils, and they were not allowed to play any part in the life of the nation. They were seen only as enigmatic figures, dressed in their gorgeous robes, when they celebrated the divine offices. The external pomp which surrounded them emphasised their helplessness and isolation. In the East, Confirmation is administered by the priest, with oil blessed by the united Episcopate, and therefore the bishop hardly ever saw his flock, and the flock never met him except during services at the Cathedral.

The policy of rigid control and suppression, so persistently pursued by the Empire in regard to the Church and its clergy, was somewhat modified during the years when the crisis was approaching. The Government, realising its increasing alienation from the people, tried to enlist the support of the clergy and made various attempts to use them as leaders of the extreme nationalists, who were supposed to be the only force capable of opposing the revolutionaries. The response of the bishops and parish priests to this invitation to collaborate was negative. Only a few of them joined the ranks of the " Union of the Russian People ", or of the other reactionary parties sponsored by the Government. But those who did so caused a great deal of harm. They became notorious, for, while the rest had to keep silence, they were allowed to speak and to write. The impression was created that the leaders of the Russian Church were on the side of reaction and, though this did not correspond to the facts, it was a belief difficult to dispel. Those, however, who had knowledge of the internal condition of the Russian Church could not be deceived; they were aware that the unsatisfactory economic and social conditions of the clergy linked them naturally with those who wanted to see the country reformed, self-government granted, the standard of education raised and the living conditions of the peasants improved.[1]

Such were the negative features of Russian Church life. They were, however, counterbalanced by several positive achievements. The most important was the mature and responsible attitude of the lay people to their religion. The majority of Russian Christians did not make the mistake of identifying the Church with the clergy. Having been trained in the atmosphere of Orthodox Services, which are corporate actions in which priests, deacons and lay people have their own parts to perform, Russians have always been free from clericalism.[2] They loved a good and faithful pastor but, when they had to cope with insufficiency or failure in a priest, they ascribed it to his human frailty and prayed for the pardon of his sins.[3]

[1] One of the standard accusations in England against the Russian clergy has been their supposed opposition to popular education. This charge is a typical example of misunderstanding caused by ignorance and prejudice. The Russian Church, as a matter of fact, was deprived by the State, from the time of Peter the Great's reforms, of participation in the education of the nation, and therefore could neither hinder nor assist in this vital side of Russian life till the end of the nineteenth century.

The situation was changed since 1882–83, when the Government began to authorise and even encourage the building of parish schools. In order to show the rapid expansion of this work, two figures can be quoted. In 1886 120,000 roubles were spent yearly on church schools; by 1895 this sum had increased to 3,279,145.

It is also necessary to correct another widespread impression about the almost universal illiteracy of the Russians prior to the Communist Revolution. The last Imperial census was taken in 1897, and it showed that not more than 20% of the miscellaneous inhabitants of the Empire could read and write. This high proportion of illiterates was due to the vast number of old people who had not yet been affected by the primary schools introduced in ever-increasing numbers by the popularly elected provincial and district Councils (*Zemstvo*) since 1864. It is therefore more instructive to study the figures of the recruits into the army. In 1897, 53% of the young men were literate; in 1913 75% could read and write. A partial census taken in 1920 revealed that on the eve of the Communist experiment 79% of the men and 44% of the women in Russia were literate. The Russian Parliament (*Duma*) passed in 1912 a law enforcing universal education, and it was calculated that by 1920 all the children of the various nationalities of the Russian Empire would be supplied with schools and teachers. The first world war and the revolution retarded the realisation of this plan for some fifteen years.

[2] See N. Zernov, *The Church of the Eastern Christians*, pp. 63–72.

[3] An example of this attitude was given in an article published in one of the anti-religious magazines in Soviet Russia. Its author, one of the anti-religious instructors, relates the following incident: He gave to a village congregation an eloquent description of some of the unworthy priests. The effect of this talk was not quite what the speaker expected. The audience asked many questions, and at the end of the lecture a woman, who was particularly keen to know the details of the priests' failings, thanked the speaker and added: "Now we know better how many difficulties and temptations hinder their work and we'll pray more warmly to God to pardon and help our pastors."

The Russian clergy, in their precarious financial position, were often unable to alleviate the temporal needs of their parishioners, but the laity did not expect any material assistance from them, for it never looked upon the Church as a philanthropic society run by the well-to-do for the benefit of the poor. The destitute and downtrodden members of the congregation felt that they held the privileged position in the Church of Christ, for the Kingdom of God was closer to them than to those who enjoyed power and riches.

Maurice Baring, who had many opportunities of observing Russian people, on the eve of the Empire's collapse said, " Their Church smells of the poor ", and it was true, for the Church was their refuge and consolation, and they were entirely at home at its services. Russian Christians were aware that their Church was handicapped in its work, that their clergy were often too much preoccupied with their daily worries, and that some of the monks and nuns failed to live up to their high vocation; but neither were they themselves free from the same sins nor from the control of the same State officials who kept the Church silent and immobile. But whatever the failures and limitations of the Church, it belonged to the people and not to the State or to the upper classes. Russian history contains many examples of the deep devotion of the common people to Christianity. The most striking among them is provided by the Old Believers, those Christians who refused to accept Nikon's reforms and Peter's scheme for subjugating the Church. When they separated from the main body in the seventeenth century, they considered themselves to be the faithful remnant of the true Church, and therefore they had every intention of preserving intact the whole traditional expression of Christian life, including the threefold ministry. The bishops who sided with them were, however, arrested and had no time to ordain successors, and the Old Believers found themselves without an episcopate. It was a great shock to them, but the lay people decided to carry on until such time as a bishop could join their ranks and restore the lawful hierarchy. They had to wait for two hundred years, but, in the nineteenth century, they at last secured a bishop and revived in their midst a full sacramental life. The Old Believers provide a unique example of a denomination run for centuries by laymen who never assumed the functions of the ministers, because they firmly believed in the vital necessity of Episcopal ordinations.

The history of the Russian Church in the twentieth century offers further illustration of the same keenness on the part of the laity, who took a prominent part in various attempts to recover for the Church its freedom of action. The lay leaders of that period belonged originally to two distinct circles, but they were soon united in enlightened and convinced support of the long-delayed reforms.

One of these groups was composed of the teaching staff of the Academies, the centres of higher theological learning. It included several outstanding laymen, for example, a professor of Moral Theology, M. N. Tareev (1866–1934), a historian, Vassili Bolotov (1853–1900), a philosopher, V. I. Nesmelov (d. 1920), Anton Kartashev (d. 1960) and several others. These men found encouragement and support among the intelligentsia, some of whom began to turn their attention to the spiritual resources of their own culture and repudiated their former uncritical admiration of the West. This movement for return to the Church amongst the intellectual and artistic élite had, however, no time to affect the bulk of their class, which, up to the outburst of the Revolution, remained indifferent to and ignorant of Christianity.

The following were some of the best-known men who became concerned with the destiny of the Russian Church: the philosopher V. S. Soloviev (1853–1900), Prince Sergei Trubetskoi, Rector of Moscow University (1862–1905), and his brothers, Evgeni (1863–1920) and Grigori (1872–1930); P. N. Novgorodtsev (1866–1924), professor of Law, S. N. Bulgakov (1871–1944), professor of Economics, and P. B. Struve (1870–1944); the philosophers S. L. Frank (d. 1950), N. A. Berdyaev (d. 1948) and V. F. Ern (1879–1917); the journalist V. V. Rozanov (1856–1919);[1] the writers D. S. Merezhkovski (1865–1941), B. Zaitsev (b. 1881), A. M. Remizov (d. 1957); the poets Zinaida Hippius (d. 1945), Viacheslav Ivanov (d. 1949), Alexander Blok (1880–1921), Andrei Bely (1880–1935) and Maximilian Voloshin (1877–1933).

Some of them re-discovered the spiritual treasures of the Church and, like Sergei Bulgakov and his friend Pavel Florenski,[2] were ordained priests. Others were not able to find the way to the Mother Church and remained on the fringe of historical Christianity. As an expression of the search for the Christian

[1] See V. Rozanov, Solitaria, London, 1927.
[2] One of the leading Russian theologians of the twentieth century. The author of the book, The Pillar and Foundation of Truth.

answer to life, religious philosophical study circles were started
in the University cities. The best known of them was that of
St. Petersburg (1901–3), at which, for the first time, representatives of the clergy and of the Intelligentsia met each other and
heatedly debated questions vital to both sides. Its president was
Bishop Sergius (1867–1944), who was elected Patriarch in 1943.

The new interest in Christianity was a part of the movement
of awakening in which the nation was caught in those years.
1904–6 was a period of important reforms which had many
repercussions in the life of the Church. The new era of political
and religious freedom at last released the Church from its long
captivity, and a flood of uncensored articles inundated the pages
of religious periodicals and of the secular press, expressing the
true mind of Russian Christians.

The Imperial Decree of 1905, granting religious freedom to
all citizens, was particularly welcomed by the majority of Church
people. Their sentiment was expressed in a letter signed by
thirty-two priests of St. Petersburg and published in the *Church
Messenger*, the official organ of their diocese (N11. 17 March,
1905). These priests wrote: " The forthcoming liberation of
the religious conscience from external restraints . . . is welcomed with great joy by all true members of the Orthodox
Church. . . . The Church is at last acquitted of the heavy
charge of violating and suppressing religious freedom. This was
formerly done in her name, under the pretence of supporting her,
but it was done against her will and against her spirit. . . . The
time has come for the Church to resume her proper influence in
all spheres of national life, and this can be done by a return to
the traditional canonical order, based on self-government and
independence of the State. This can only be achieved by the
convocation of a Council of the whole Russian Church."

The demand for the Council and for the liberation of the
Church from State control was so widespread that, out of sixty-
three diocesan bishops who were asked to give their opinion on
this point, sixty-one stated that they welcomed the reforms, and
yet all these bishops had been appointed under Pobedonostsev's
rule, from the ranks of the more obedient clergy.[1] The feeling
of many bishops was expressed by Bishop Antonin of Narva,
who, in an article published in the conservative paper *Novoe*

---

[1] See N. Zernov, " The Russian Episcopate and Church Reform " (*Church
Quarterly Review*, April 1934).

Vremia (March 20th, 1905), wrote: " The gates are thrown open, the procession of the nation's representatives is approaching the palace of the State " (he is referring to the impending Convocation of the Parliament—" Duma "); " with fear and anxiety, the Orthodox wait to see whether the Apostle Paul will come forth once again chained to the arm of a Roman centurion."

Because of this general demand for freedom, the Government was obliged to make several concessions to the Church. Pobedonostsev was forced to retire in 1905. The convocation of the Council was promised, and a commission was set up to prepare the Constitution and agenda for the ecclesiastical gathering. The commission suggested an impressive list of improvements, chiefly concerned with the restoration of self-government to the Church, and with its full share in social and educational activities. Much attention was given to the raising of the economic standard of the clergy and to the reorganisation of the seminaries. The revival of the diaconate for women was also contemplated. This return to the ancient practice of the Eastern Church was strongly advocated by several theologians, like Professor S. Troitski, and the Abbess Ekaterina of Liesna (1850–1925), the ablest Russian woman theologian of her time.

But the bright hopes of these years did not last long. The temporary concessions made by the Government were withdrawn as soon as the political reaction set in. After two years of comparative freedom, the Church was reduced to its former impotence and silence. The Empire fought till its last breath against Christian liberty, and only after its fall did the all-Russian Church Council meet in Moscow, in August 1917.

The last years of the Empire were overshadowed by the mysterious figure of the lay-Elder Grigori Rasputin (*d.* 1916). Owing to the lack of knowledge about the Russian Church, he is usually described, by Western writers, as a monk. Some even quote him as an example of the supposedly corrupt clericalism of the Orthodox Church. Whatever were the moral faults of Rasputin's character, his case has no bearing upon the alleged deficiency of the Russian clergy, for Rasputin was neither priest, nor monk, but an ordinary married peasant.[1] Besides, his spiritual background had more in common with the mystical

---

[1] One of his daughters, Maria, who migrated to the U.S.A., has tried to vindicate in several books her father's reputation: *The Real Rasputin*, London, 1929; *My Father*, London, 1934.

sect of Khlysty [1] than with the tradition of the Church. The source of his influence and power lay in facts precisely opposite to those which are usually put forward in popular literature on Russia.   In no sense did Rasputin represent Russian clericalism; he was listened to by the Empress because she believed him to be the genuine spokesman of the millions of Russian peasants— it was with them that the rulers of the Empire were anxious to restore the contact which had been lost since the time of Peter the Great.   It was too late, however.   The peasant who came to St. Petersburg and took a place of honour near the throne was not the sound Orthodox Christian that some of his admirers believed him to be.   He was a man endowed with a striking personality and with gifts of healing, but he was possessed by lust and dark passions, and his fall dragged down those who had received him as an inspired prophet.

The Empire suddenly collapsed in March 1917.   It fell as an old tree falls, rotted at the heart by weather and time.   The drastic change in the traditional political order, wrought in the midst of a long and exhausting war, created complete chaos in the country.   The Russians passed through a period of dis-integration similar to that experienced by them in the " Time of Troubles ".   Everyone thought himself released from any obligations to the rest of the community.   The Government fell at first into the hands of Westernised liberals.   Their political programme, borrowed from Europe, had no roots in Russian life; their ideals and aspirations and the outlook of the peasants had nothing in common.   The new Government had no authority, its orders were disobeyed, and within a few months the great country was the hopeless prey of anarchy and civil war.

The fact that a considerable part of Russia's territory was over-run in 1917 by the foreign invader only completed the parallel between the early stages of the Russian Revolution of the twentieth century and the troubles that followed the end of the dynasty of Rurik 300 years earlier.

It is remarkable that the first signs of recovery during those two great crises appeared among the same classes of Russian people and in the same district.   As, in the " Time of Troubles ", the Northern and Eastern Provinces, which had escaped the dis-

[1] Khlysty is a sect which teaches that it is permissible to overcome the temptations of the flesh by yielding temporarily to them.

integrating influence of serfdom, were the first to resist the anarchy, so, in the 1917–19 period, the north and east, including Siberia, and also the south, inhabited by the freedom-loving Cossacks, preserved social order more efficiently, whilst the central region collapsed completely. The upper classes on both occasions proved inadequate to their task and failed to direct the will of the nation, whilst statesmanship and common sense were displayed mostly by small traders and peasants in the provinces which enjoyed a higher standard of economic prosperity.

But the parallel between these two Russian revolutions ends here, for a new and powerful factor entered on the scene in the autumn of 1917, which was absent three centuries ago. This was the appearance of a small but well-organised group of International Communists.[1]

In the seventeenth century the Russians themselves restored order in the country, through the free co-operation of local self-governing communities. This process started also in 1917, but its course was interrupted by another revolution—the seizure of power by Lenin and Trotsky, who proclaimed their party's dictatorship over the Russian people and started ruthlessly to remould the life of the country in accordance with the doctrines of Marxian Communism. They were bitterly hostile to all Russia's past, and especially uncompromising to every form of religion. The end of the St. Petersburg Empire therefore meant for the nation not the return to their traditional order, but a further compulsory Westernisation on an unprecedented scale and with unprecedented speed.

Before this new revolution was complete, the Church happily had recovered its independence, and it met therefore the Communist assault as a free and self-governing body. This all-important achievement was due to a large extent to the foresight, energy and courage of Prof. Anton Kartashev, who in the June of 1917 became Minister of Religion in the Cabinet of the Temporary Government. He refused to accept the title of Procurator of the Synod, and by this act clearly indicated his determination to bring to an end the order established by Peter the Great.

[1] The tension between the international and national tendencies within the Communist party came to an open clash after Lenin's death in 1924. Trotsky and his supporters who represented International Marxism were expelled from the party in the course of 1926–28. In 1929 Trotsky was deported from Russia ; the rest of his followers suffered severe punishment and ceased to exist as a distinct group.

He realised the critical state of the country, and, overcoming enormous obstacles, helped to assemble in Moscow the freely-elected Council of the Russian Church.

In 1917, the country was intoxicated by the air of freedom; meetings, conferences, open debates became the passion of the people. But among all those ephemeral gatherings the only one which left a permanent trace was the Church Council which assembled in Moscow on August 15th, 1917. It consisted of 564 members, including 278 lay representatives. It was a feat of organising ability to bring together from the remotest parts of the country such a large number of people at a time when the nation was in the grip of war and revolution. It was a proof of the maturity and ability of the Christians that they were able, after an interval of 200 years, during which no Councils had been held, to proceed in good order to elect new organs of Church administration and to restore the self-government that the Germanised Empire had taken away.

The traditionally popular character of Eastern Christianity helped the Russians to redress the evils in their badly shaken Church, and they did this under the most adverse conditions and in a surprisingly short time. The success of the Council stands out as particularly striking in comparison with the utter failure of the Constitutional Assembly, which was elected in accordance with the most up-do-date Western democratic methods and was dispersed by a handful of Communists. The members of the Church were one body, but the people of Russia had no political cohesion. High passions and class antagonisms, which reigned supreme all over the country, could not of course be barred altogether from the meetings of the Council. The conservative and the more radical elements clashed frequently at its sessions; the point of their contention, however, was neither doctrine nor worship, but the practical ways of restoring full autonomy to the Church. Some of the members of the Council stood for the revival of the Patriarchate, others advocated the formation of a collegiate body, objecting to the rule of a single man.

The Communist uprising in October 1917 and the realisation that a period of hard trials was at hand silenced all differences, and on November 5th, 1917, Tikhon, the Metropolitan of Moscow, was elected to the Patriarchal Throne. According to the charter drawn up by the Council, the Patriarch had to exercise his power in harmony with administrative bodies elected by the National Council and he was responsible to it. For the first time in its history, the Russian Church acquired a proper canonical organisation, but it had no time to put it into practice, for the wave of revolution swept away all the carefully worded resolutions and left the Church wretched and poverty-stricken in face of new and formidable enemies who were determined to bring Christianity, and, indeed, all forms of religion, to a speedy end.

CHAPTER XVII

THE CHRISTIANS AND THE GODLESS

SUPPRESSION of Christians in any civilised country would have seemed inconceivable before the outbreak of the Russian Revolution in 1917. When, therefore, the Communists launched their attack on the Church, they opened a new period in the history of the world, yet few people had sufficient foresight or courage to recognise the true meaning of this momentous event. The majority of Western Christians, blinded by their prejudice against the Eastern Church, confused by their ignorance and fear of Russia, found a refuge in the comforting conviction that the conflict in Russia was local and had no bearing upon the destiny of Christianity as a whole. Russia was conveniently classified as a semi-barbaric country with a corrupt form of religion, and the conflict was explained as a relapse into the dark ages. In reality, it was a decisive step towards the creation of a new order. The origin of the struggle between Christians and atheists in Russia, with its world-wide significance, lies not so much in peculiarly Russian social conditions, as mainly in the irreconcilability of the Christian doctrine of man as a servant of the living God and the modern belief that man is self-sufficient.

The fact that the clash between these two beliefs took place, not in one of the leading European countries, but in remote and unknown Russia, greatly confused the issue; so that only slowly and reluctantly did Western Christendom become aware of the reasons which lay behind the Communists' determination to stamp out any belief in God in every land under their control. Yet neither Karl Marx (d. 1883) nor his disciple, V. Lenin (d. 1924) had ever made any secret about their resolute opposition to any revealed religion. As soon as the Communists were triumphant in Russia they began to apply the doctrines of their teachers to all spheres of life, firmly believing in their absolute truth.

The Communist experiment in Russia was the last and most radical stage in the process of imitation of the West inaugurated by Peter the Great. For more than 200 years, the upper section of Russian society had blindly followed the lead of Europe, convinced that all available wisdom and truth were contained in the theories and methods of civilised Western nations. Lenin was one of the most ardent exponents of this point of view. He treated Karl Marx's doctrines as the final revelation of truth—they were not only a political theory to him, but a new, scientific religion, capable of solving all the problems of life and, therefore, intolerant of any rival teachings. Lenin wrote: " The genius of Marx lies exactly in the fact that he provided the answers to questions put by the leading thinkers of mankind. . . . His teaching is so powerful because it is true. It is complete and systematic and gives to people an integral world view. . . . Materialism turned out to be the only consistent philosophy true to all the teachings of natural science and inimical to superstition and magic." [1] For Lenin, Marxism was so attractive because it gathered up all the finest fruits of European civilisation. He described it as " the lawful successor of the best that mankind created in the nineteenth century, in German Philosophy, English Political Economy and French Socialism." [2] The creative genius of the three most advanced European countries, the last word in the evolution of emancipated man, was contained, according to Lenin, in the books of the greatest of all prophets.

Russian Christians, in 1917, came up against a vigorous force, which had been created not in their own country or in their own tradition, but in the secularised West, and which had found its leader in a German Jew who had made his home in England. Karl Marx combined in himself the massive learning of a German scholar with the ardent faith of a Jewish prophet. He made an exhaustive study of economics, collected a vast array of figures and statistics, and arrived at the conclusion that mankind was subjected to the iron rule of economic necessity. He inflicted a heavy blow upon the optimistic liberalism of the nineteenth century with its trust in reason and the creative genius of emancipated man. But Marx was not a pessimist. He believed in a Messiah, the deliverer of the suffering human race from its economic chains. He promised to his followers that the time would come when people would be free and enjoy universal prosperity. This Jewish millennium he associated with

[1] Lenin, *Three Sources and Three Essential Elements of Marxism*, 1913.
[2] *Ibid.*

the victory of the proletariat, the collective Messiah of the future, the " suffering servant " of the proud and selfish wealthier classes.

Marx was an atheist. But though he denied the existence of the Creator, he still believed in the redemption of the world, and he drew a sharp line between good and evil. The strange mixture of scholarship and prophecy in his writings, his ardent love of freedom, and his acceptance of the irrevocable laws of economics, his materialism and his faith in the coming trans-figuration of man and the Universe, made his teaching par-ticularly attractive to the Westernised Russian revolutionaries. It not only pleased their ambitions to be exponents of the last word in European radicalism, it also satisfied their longing for an integral outlook and for social justice which they had inherited from their Christian past. Marx and Russian radicals met on Biblical ground, for though they both denied the truth of the Bible, nevertheless they had been fed from the same source of divine revelation. Marx's hatred of oppression and his faith in the triumph of righteousness and freedom are incomprehensible to those who have not been imbued with Biblical ideas. Karl Marx had many disciples in the West, but only his Russian followers put his teaching into practice. This was not due to the economic readiness of the country for this experiment. Russia was the least suitable land for Communism from an industrial point of view but the Russians had faith, and that was the force which was lacking among other European Socialists.

One can understand Russian Communism only if one realises that it is not merely an economic and social experiment, but also one of the greatest religious revolutions in the history of mankind, carried through by a group of men knowing no other truth than dialectic materialism, and recognising no other prophet than Karl Marx. Sceptics and egoists cannot be made into good revolutionaries. People without hope in the ultimate victory of righteousness are unable to sacrifice their security for the unknown future. The rest of Europe had lost the ardour of the belief in God, but, equally, it had not the courage boldly to deny His existence. This was not the case with the Russians. They split into two opposite camps and fought the battle for and against God till the finish.

The story of the conflict between atheists and Christians in Russia is of absorbing interest, for it reveals the strength and the weakness of atheism, as well as the essential and non-essential

elements in the Christian religion. It is vital to remember,
however, that the clash in Russia occurred neither between
the Church and the State, as in the French Revolution, nor
between Christianity and revived paganism, as in Hitler's Germany, but between those who denied and those who asserted the
existence of God. Every form of faith in Him was assaulted,[1]
but, because the vast majority of believers in Russia were members
of the Orthodox Church, that body had to sustain the main
weight of the attack. The godless literature published by the
Communists in Russia has never failed to emphasise the universal
character of this struggle. Roman Catholics, Anglicans, Protestants, as well as believing Jews and Mahometans, have all been the
butt of their criticism.

Five stages are discernible in this contest, and each of them
brought the opponents to a clearer realisation of their relative
strength. At first the godless were optimistic; their materialism
blinded them to the true nature of Christianity, and they thought
that by destroying the economic foundations of the Church
they could bring about the collapse of the whole building. They
also had a naïve faith in science, trusting that its data have con-
clusively proved that God does not exist, and that man is nothing
more than a piece of highly organised matter. Therefore, the
first law drafted by Lenin in 1918 allowed both religious and
anti-religious propaganda, and its main weapon against the
Church was the confiscation of all its property. The Communists expected a speedy collapse of Christianity as the result of
this action, but, to their astonishment, the Church, deprived of its
material resources, deserted by its half-hearted members, gained
new vitality and power. During the first period (1918–22), the
country was rent asunder by anarchy and civil war, and many
clergy and faithful laity perished, but the Church remained
relatively free and there was little systematic persecution.
Christian leaders at that time had no idea of the character of
their adversary; they still thought of the Communists as usurpers
who, with the help of criminal elements, had temporarily seized
control of the country in order to pillage it and surrender it to
foreign enemies, an idea which gained ground by the defeatist
campaign conducted by the Bolsheviks during the first world war

---

[1] See the conclusions at which Paul Anderson arrived on p. 103, in *People,
Church and State in Modern Russia*, S.C.M. Press, 1944. Mr. Anderson is one
of the world's experts on the religious situation in Russia.

and by the separate peace which Lenin hastily concluded with Germany in 1918. The other face of Communism, its integral philosophy of life, its programme of far-reaching social and economic reforms, was still concealed from the Russian Christians. The Patriarch, Tikhon, tried to protect the Church by issuing, in 1918, a writ of excommunication against all those who attacked Christians and profaned church buildings, but he soon realised the uselessness of such a weapon. Those who fought against him assaulted not the Church, but God, and the threat of divine punishment only excited their anti-religious fervour.

The second period in the struggle opened in 1922 and lasted until 1929. The godless realised, at last, that the Church could not be destroyed merely by confiscation of its property and the exile of individual Christians. They therefore changed their tactics, and attempted to undermine its influence by splitting believers into hostile factions. At the same time they offered privileges to all dissenters and sectarians. The Patriarch Tikhon was suddenly arrested on August 5th, 1922. Seven days later a group of priests were allowed to visit him in prison, and they obtained from the Patriarch permission to take over temporarily the ecclesiastical administration till the arrival in Moscow of his deputy, the Metropolitan Agathangel. This transfer was a part of a carefully arranged plan. The priests had no intention of handing over the government of the Church to the Patriarch's nominee; instead they convoked a Council (August 1922), and announced various reforms the chief of which was the introduction of a married Episcopate.[1] The Patriarch was harshly criticised for his anti-government policy, and the new leaders, who called themselves members of the Living Church, or the " Renewed Church ", declared that they were ready to support Communism, because it put into practice the social message of the Gospel. At first the plot succeeded well. Utter confusion reigned in the Church; many leading bishops, including the future Patriarch Sergius, accepted the new ecclesiastical government, and the majority of the parishes went over to the Living Church, knowing nothing about the inner story of the movement. The Soviet Government meanwhile granted several concessions to the rebels. They were allowed to open a theological college

---

[1] From the seventh century the bishops of the Eastern Church have been recruited from the ranks of monks or widowed clergy, whilst the parish priests have been expected to marry.

and to print literature, on condition that it contained incriminations and attacks on the other sections of the Church. In April and May 1923 a second Council was held in Moscow. This time unmistakable signs of disintegration became apparent. The leaders of the Living Church were mostly ambitious men who sought their own interests at a time when other Christians had to suffer. They split into several competing factions. Their violent hostility to the imprisoned Patriarch, whom they deposed at their second Council, alienated many of their supporters, whilst the Communists themselves showed nothing but contempt for their unwanted allies. The official Press made it clear that, in the eyes of the atheists, the Living Church was in no way better than the Church of the Patriarch. Any idea of compromise between dialectical materialism and belief in God was abhorrent to members of the Party.

The next blow was inflicted upon the dissenting bodies by Tikhon's unexpected release from prison in June 1923. Simultaneously with this grant of freedom a statement under the Patriarch's signature was published in the newspaper *Isvestia* on June 27th, 1923. In it, Tikhon declared his loyalty to the Soviet Government and confessed his mistake in condemning the Brest-Litovsk separate peace-treaty with Germany in 1918. He also publicly expressed regret for his opposition to the confiscation of the sacred vessels in 1922. This act of surrender shocked some Christians, but the majority considered that the Patriarch was thereby taking upon himself the cross of self-abasement for the sake of his flock, and they accepted his action. Till his death on April 7th, 1925, Tikhon was surrounded by the warm affection of all the faithful. The attempt to undermine the solidarity of the Church had failed; only a small minority adhered to the Living Church and to the other dissenting bodies which were to hold their third and last Council in October 1926.

The lesson of this second stage of the conflict was learned by both parties. The godless realised that neither material hardships nor government-instigated divisions were sufficient to destroy Christianity. The leaders of the Church understood that the Soviet Government was firmly established and that the Christians would have to find a new way of life under the rule of the resolute enemies of their religion.

The most important statement from the Christians, at that time, was an open letter, composed in 1926 by a group of Russian

Churchmen who were imprisoned in the concentration camp on the Solovetski Island. These confessors, with calm dignity, made it clear in their epistle that they were not involved in any political struggle against the new social order. The cause of the conflict between the Christians and the Soviet State was the incompatibility of the teaching of the Church with the materialistic and godless philosophy of the Communist Party.

" The Church ", they wrote, " recognises the existence of the spiritual principle; communism denies it. The Church believes in the Living God, Creator of the world, Guide of its life; communism does not admit His existence. . . . The Church believes in the steadfast principles of morality, justice and law; communism looks upon them as the conditional results of class struggle, and values moral questions only from the standpoint of their usefulness. The Church instils the feeling that humility elevates man's soul; communism abases man through pride."

The conclusion reached by the authors was that Christians, in the existing circumstances, wished for nothing other than the complete and systematic application of the law which separated the Church from the State. They were prepared to bear any amount of poverty, to work under any restrictions, for they were sure by that time that no power on earth could destroy the seeds of Christian faith as long as there were men who believed in the truth of the Gospel. These words, written by those who fearlessly faced suffering and death, represented the opinion of an important party within the Orthodox Church, but there was another school of thought, whose spokesmen were Metropolitan Sergius (Stragorodsky, who at that time held the office of the vice-locum tenens of the Patriarchal Throne) and two young and energetic bishops, Alexis (Simansky, the future Patriarch) and Nicolas (Iarushevich). They believed that it was impractical to expect a genuine separation of Church and State and that the ecclesiastical leaders had to search for some compromise and accommodation with even a hostile Government. The outcome of the negotiations between this group of bishops and the Communists was a declaration issued in 1927 by Metropolitan Sergius in which he not only reiterated the pledge of loyalty to the Soviet State but went further by proclaiming that the aspirations of the Church and of the Government were identical. He added also that the Church had not been oppressed nor persecuted.

As a reward the Communists agreed to " register " the Ortho-

dox Church and restore its proper organisation, a right which had
been denied to it since 1922. Metropolitan Sergius's declaration
was a step with far-reaching consequences for the fate of the Russian Church. Since 1927 the official pronouncements of the
Russian Orthodox hierarchy have adopted the language of Soviet
propaganda and repeated the lies which form such an integral part
of Communist totalitarianism.

This document profoundly disturbed and split the Orthodox
community. Some believed that the method chosen by Sergius
was wrong; others thought that he had no other means of preserving the public life of the Church. The immediate result of this
action was the formation of several conflicting groups under different Russian hierarchs: the majority accepted Sergius's leadership,
but others repudiated it or remained uncommitted.

These tensions soon lost their acuteness, for the Church entered
the third and most tragic period of its history. During it all Christian groups without any exception were exposed to a violent
onslaught from the godless State. It started on April 8th, 1929,
when a revised law on religion was published by Stalin. This
time every form of religious propaganda was made a legal
offence.[1] Moreover, Article 17 prohibited also every form of
philanthropic and educational activity, and the life of the
Church was limited strictly to the conduct of divine worship.

Article 17 reads as follows:—

" Religious unions (parishes) are forbidden, (a) to establish
mutual aid funds, co-operative and productive unions, and in
general, to use the property at their disposal for any other purpose than the satisfying of religious needs; (b) to give material
aid to their members; to organize either special meetings for
children, youth, women, for prayer and other purposes, or
general meetings, groups, circles, departments, Biblical or literary,
handwork for labour, religious study, etc., and also to organize
excursions and children's playgrounds; to open libraries, reading
rooms, to organize sanatoria and medical aid. Only such books
as are necessary for the performance of services are permitted
in the Church buildings and houses of prayer."

This new law marked a radical departure from the first
optimistic expectations of the godless. In 1918, they confidently

[1] These prohibitions have been reinstated in Article 124 of Stalin's Constitution of 1936, which states that " Freedom for the conduct of religious
worship and freedom for anti-religious propaganda is recognised for all citizens."

believed in their ability to win people to atheism by force of
argument in open debate.   Lenin therefore granted without
hesitation, to all citizens, the freedom to indulge in both religious
and anti-religious propaganda.   In 1929, after eleven years of
struggle, the leaders of the atheist movement knew better than
their teacher that the Christians had arguments at their disposal
which were stronger than those familiar to the godless.   They
realised that the best way to defeat religion was to keep the believers' mouths shut.   The Christians were such formidable
opponents that only by being deprived of every means of self-
defence could they be crushed.   At first the Leninists concentrated
their efforts on the anti-religious propaganda.   The schools
especially became the strongholds of anti-god teaching, whilst any
attempt to counteract the compulsory atheism was ruthlessly suppressed.   Yet even these measures proved to be ineffectual and the
Government soon embarked on a wholesale destruction of church
buildings and a mass deportation of clergy and leading members of
congregations.   This unprecedented persecution had periods of
intensification.   One of them was in 1932, when in Petersburg
alone thirty churches were pulled down in the course of three
months.   (In this city out of ninety-six churches standing before
the Revolution only seven remain today.)   Another crucial time
was 1936–7 when the number of people condemned to slave labour
in the extermination camps reached the unbelievable figure of between fifteen and twenty million people.   In these two years the
Russian episcopate was almost liquidated—more than seventy
bishops were deported and perished in the camps, only four remaining free.   The life of the Christian Church seemed to come to
an end.   Stalin felt so confident of his victory that the census of
1936 included a question about religious allegiance.   The Soviet
press promised to its readers that the census would reveal the overwhelming atheism of the population.   The government apparently
suffered an unpleasant surprise as the results of this census were
completely suppressed.   The next census, taken a little later, did
not include the question of religious allegiance.

Nevertheless many foreign observers had at that time the impression that the Communists had succeeded in breaking down
traditional Orthodoxy and that, if religious freedom were ever
restored, Christianity in Russia would take a new shape vastly
different from the old.   The next and fourth period of the history
of the Russian Church has completely overturned this view.

CHAPTER XVIII

THE RUSSIAN CHURCH DURING AND AFTER THE SECOND WORLD WAR

SUNDAY, June 21st, 1941 is one of the turning-points in the history of the world. On that day the German armies invaded Soviet territory. Hitler chose for his attack the very date on which, in 1812, Napoleon had crossed the frontier of the Russian Empire. Both acts were fatal to the aggressor. The victory of the anti-Hitler alliance had many far-reaching repercussions, but one of the most ominous was the extension of Stalin's power over central and eastern Europe.

That date—June 21st, 1941—has a special significance for Russian Christians, for in that year it was the Sunday on which they remember all the saints of their land.[1] Was it a mere coincidence that the events of June 21st and the national emergency which followed led to a drastic reversal of Stalin's religious policy and so to the restoration of the Russian Church as an articulate and organised body? For Russian believers it meant that Russian saints were with them in this war which cost Russia over twenty million lives. In their gigantic struggle people needed religion.

By September 1941 anti-religious propaganda came to an abrupt end. The Society of the Godless was disbanded. In 1942 the Government published fifty thousand copies of a luxuriously produced and lavishly illustrated book with the ambitious title *The Truth about Religion in Russia*; its purpose being to demonstrate Stalin's benevolent attitude towards believers. Several factors contributed towards this reorientation, which marked the fourth stage of the conflict between Christians and Communists. Metropolitan Sergius from the very first day of hostilities took an uncompromising attitude of whole-hearted support for the war effort. His appeals to patriotism met with popular response and such churches as were still open were crowded with worshippers praying for their suffering country. It became clear that freer expression of religious feeling would unite believer and unbeliever behind the Government.

[1] Russian Saints' Day always falls on the second Sunday after Whit Sunday.

163

The Kremlin also could not ignore the significance of the revival of church life in the territories occupied by the Germans, a revival which has been described as " general, massive and spontaneous". As soon as the Communist authorities fled, townsmen and villagers took into their own hands the reopening and restoration of churches. The people thronged to the sacraments, thousands were baptised, married and received Holy Communion. The following figures illustrate the extent of the revival: the Kiev diocese had in 1914 1,770 churches, served by 1,437 priests, and 23 religious houses; in 1940 there were only 2 churches served by 3 priests, and no monasteries. The statistics of 1942–3 show up to 500 churches, some 600 priests (300 of them newly ordained) and 8 religious houses. The reappearance of monastic life is particularly impressive after years of atheistic propaganda.

The war revealed the hold of religion on the Russian people and the Government could no longer disregard this fact. On September 4th, 1943 Stalin received a delegation of the Russian Church, consisting of Metropolitans Sergius, Alexis and Nicolas, the three authors of the *Concordat* of 1927. After sixteen years of delay the Soviet dictator fulfilled the original promise and sanctioned the restoration of the Patriarchate. On September 7th the nineteen bishops who returned from concentration camps acclaimed Metropolitan Sergius as Patriarch, and after his death in 1944 a church assembly, consisting this time of 170 delegates (bishops, priests and laymen), met in 1945 to declare Metropolitan Alexis his successor. In return for recognition the church hierarchy had to support Stalin's foreign policy. Metropolitan Nicolas, eloquent and dynamic, became ambassador-at-large to the Moscow Patriarchate, and took a leading part in various international and interdenominational conferences, skilfully defending the Soviet aims.

Since the restoration of the Patriarchate the main agonising dilemma confronting the Russian Church has been the structure of its government. It is highly centralised at present and maintains effectively the unity of the Church. At the same time it gives to the agents of the State the possibility of a strict control over the entire ecclesiastical administration. There have been voices claiming that decentralisation could secure greater independence, but it would also jeopardise the unity so essential in the times of troubles. The paradox is that this unity is purchased by the official denial of persecution. Yet it is the prayers and example of innumerable martyrs and confessors which keep alive the Russian Church.

The post-war years witnessed a further consolidation of the Church.   The following statistics[1] illustrate this:

	In 1914	In 1939	In 1953
Dioceses	73	?	73
Bishops	163	?	74
Parish clergy	51,000	some 100s	about 20,000
Monasteries	1,025	0	67
Theological schools	61	0	10

In Stalin's eyes the Church ceased to be enemy number one. He had other more urgent problems: to suppress the spirit of independence engendered by military victories and to erect an Iron Curtain designed to isolate those under his control from all contacts with the West.   One of the consequences of this was that the Consultation of the heads of the Orthodox Churches, convoked in Moscow in 1948, passed hostile resolutions against both the Vatican and the Ecumenical movement.[2]

The interregnum which followed Stalin's death in 1953 favoured the life of the Orthodox Church.   The change in Soviet foreign policy made it possible for the Moscow Patriarchate to open friendly relations with the World Council of Churches.

In 1958 Nikita Khruschev (d. 1971) assumed the mantle of charismatic leader.   He vigorously pursued a policy of de-Stalinisation; he released millions of prisoners from concentration camps and posthumously rehabilitated thousands of Stalin's victims. Yet at that time of apparent liberalisation he launched a sudden and unexpected attack on the Church, and thus began the fifth stage in the relations between Christians and Government.   The reasons for this persecution are still a question of debate, but it appears that one of the leading roles in the drama was played by Catherine Furzeva, the great favourite of the volatile dictator.   To this ambitious woman's tender mercies Khruschev entrusted the culture of the Soviet Union.   She seemed determined to succeed in the difficult area of anti-religious activity where so many of her male predecessors suffered defeat.   This promoter of culture managed to destroy more than ten thousand churches, including

---

[1] These figures are taken from Trevor Beeson's *Discretion and Valour* (Fontana 1974), p. 53.
[2] The majority of those present at the Consultation represented Churches under Communist control.

some of those classified as " historical and artistic monuments ".
As a result the number of churches used for worship fell from 18,000
in 1957 to 7,500 in 1966, the number of parish clergy from about
20,000 to 10,000, of monasteries from 67 to 16, and of theological
schools from 10 to 5.   Large areas of the country were once again
deprived of centres of worship.

This persecution was not accompanied, as under Stalin, by
arrests and deportation; the clergy were simply forced to abandon
their active ministry.   The most prominent victim of the campaign
was the famous Metropolitan Nicolas.   He tried to protest, and
was punished.   In June 1960 the Synod, under Government
pressure, " released " him from his duties as Metropolitan and from
all other offices, and in December 1961 he died in mysterious circumstances.   So ended tragically the career of a man who tried
consistently to reconcile loyalty to the Church with co-operation
with the godless State.   His successor was Nikodim (Rostov,
b. 1929, Metropolitan of Leningrad since 1965) who pursued the
same policy but with more caution.

This campaign slowed down the process of religious recovery
which had begun during the war.   It was, however, not able to
arrest it entirely.   Khruschev's fall in 1964 brought to an abrupt
end the wave of persecution.   The new Government adopted the
policy of trench warfare which expects neither rapid advance nor
precipitous retreat.   There were only a few fresh closures of
churches, but there were no reopenings.   During this period of
comparative calm the Patriarch Alexis died in 1970 at the age of 93
and in 1971 a new Council chose Pimen (Isvekov, b. 1910) as his
successor.   This Council was forced to sanction uncanonical ecclesiastical regulations which deprived the clergy of leadership in their
parishes and reduced them to the position of hired administrators
of the sacraments.

At the present time (1977) the Church in Russia is handicapped
in three ways: (a) its progress is hampered by the religious ignorance of the de-christianised population; (b) its internal life is
threatened by the infiltration of Government agents among the
clergy and parish officials; (c) its most active members, especially
among intellectual converts, are in constant danger of arrest and
incarceration in mental hospitals.   On the other hand there are
signs of hope and encouragement.   There is undoubtedly a return
to the Church among people of all walks of life including the intellectual élite; there is a growing number of fearless and dedicated

priests and laymen.   Moreover the most creative writing of contemporary Russia (such as the work of Solzhenitsyn, *b.* 1918) and
the best painting and sculpture bear the mark of religious experience
and of commitment to the teaching of the Gospel.

Study of the conflict between Communism and the Church
reveals the tenacity shown by the Party in its endeavour to exter-
minate religion.   Though the first expectations of a quick victory
were unfulfilled, the Leninists never relax the intensity of their
campaign, they only change their methods.   The official press
gives several reasons for this determination: (a) Christianity is
other-worldly and pessimistic, which undermines Marxist faith in
the cloudless future of mankind; (b) Christianity is anti-scientific,
for science has proved that God does not exist and that matter is
eternal; (c) Christian teaching of love and forgiveness hinders
social progress based on the class struggle and hatred of enemies.
The Communists are not willing to reveal the real cause of their
struggle against religion, which is the discovery by the Soviet oli-
garchy that atheists are better and more obedient material for their
totalitarian order than are Christians, who refuse to recognise the
State as the final arbiter of human destiny.   So long as the Leninists
deny men their right to follow their own convictions, so long are the
Churches sure to be oppressed and persecuted.

THE CHURCH OF RUSSIA AND THE CHRISTIAN WEST

THE Communist Revolution completed the centuries-long isolation of the Russian Church. For many years all contacts between its members and the outside world were severed, and yet the same Revolution brought about an understanding between Russian and Western Christians more profound than they had experienced in the past. There were three chief reasons for this. First, several million Orthodox Russians were forced to leave their country and look for a refuge in Europe and America. Secondly, those who remained behind were confronted by a most militant form of Western secularism and had to face its terrific challenge. And finally, the Communist experiment stimulated among other nations a widespread interest in Russia and broke down that proud sense of superiority which hitherto had characterised the attitude of the West towards Russian culture.

The appearance of the Russian Church in exile was of particular significance for the mutual re-discovery of Russian Orthodoxy and the Christian West. Until 1920, when the first wave of Russian emigrants crossed the frontier, Russians had had few occasions to meet Christians of other traditions. Only in the very early days, when Kiev was a flourishing centre of international trade, had friendly relations with the outside world been possible. The attack launched on Orthodox Russia by the Teutonic Knights in the thirteenth century, when the country was being devastated by the heathen Tartars, profoundly shocked the Russian people and revealed the West as being as hostile to them as the non-Christian East. A Russian popular song of that period described the Church of Christ as menaced by three implacable enemies, the Mahometans, the Jews, and the Latins. This feeling of hostility was further increased by the aggressive attitude of the Roman Catholics in the Ukraine and in Lithuania during their long domination over the Eastern Orthodox Church there from the fourteenth to the seventeenth centuries. Finally during the " Time of Troubles ", when the Poles overran a large part of the country and often committed acts of sacrilege in the Orthodox Churches, the whole Russian nation became convinced that nothing but antagonism could exist between it and the Western world. This sentiment was so acute that the Council of the Russian Church, in 1620, passed a resolution requiring the re-baptism of any Western Christian who wished to join the Eastern Church. The Russians, after the " Time of Troubles ", refused to see any difference between Roman Catholics and infidels. This state of mind, however, did not last long, and in the eighteenth century the Russian Church resumed the traditional Eastern recognition of baptism administered in the name of the Holy Trinity.

During the period of the Empire, the Russian Church was no longer separated from the West, as it had been under the Moscow Tsardom, but contacts remained few, and they rarely contributed to mutual understanding. In the course of the eighteenth and nineteenth centuries large territories inhabited by Roman Catholics and Protestants were incorporated in the Russian State, but no free intercourse between the representatives of these Churches was encouraged by the Imperial Government, and Christians of different traditions lived side by side, seldom mixing with one another. At the same time, the Russian theological schools maintained a purely negative attitude towards the Western Confessions; their doctrinal errors were enumerated, and that was the only side of their life which was studied. Orthodox theologians hardly ever met their opponents personally, and they conducted an abstract text-book controversy against an enemy whom no one was expected to see in the flesh. There was, of course, besides the clergy and the great bulk of Orthodox Christians, a minority of Westernised Russians who worshipped Europe and were intensely interested in every movement of Western thought. These Russians, however, had no interest in religion; they usually had only a superficial acquaintance with their own Church, and they had no desire to learn anything about the Christian tradition of the West, believing philosophy, science and economics were the sole channels leading to the discovery of truth.

There are but few instances, in the course of the nineteenth century, of the well-instructed Orthodox meeting practising members of the Western Churches on a footing of equality and respect. They include Khomiakov (d. 1860), Vladimir Soloviev (d. 1900), General Alexander Kireev (1832–1910), and a few Russian chaplains attached to embassies abroad, such as Fr. Alexei Maltsev of Berlin (d. 1916), the translator of Orthodox Service books into German, and Fr. Eugeni Smirnov of London (d. 1923). Therefore the first real meeting on any scale between Russian and Western Christians may be said to have taken place in the twentieth century.

The emigrants who came to Europe and America in 1920–22 represented a great variety of political and religious opinions. Some of them were opposed to the Communists on economic grounds; others were socialists, who had no desire to see the old Empire restored but could not accept the godlessness and ruthlessness of the new regime and preferred exile to the loss of freedom under the dictatorship of the Marxists. Most of the emigrants belonged to the intelligentsia, and the majority of them, at least nominally, were members of the Orthodox Church. Their attitude to the West was different from that shared by Russians who had visited Europe before the Revolution. These latter were admirers of the West and considered it to be that part of the world in which their social and political ideals were realised. This time the Russians had no longer the same illusions—they had no desire to stay abroad; they were forced to leave their country, and they stubbornly clung to the traditional ways of their national life.

Like the Jews in the Dispersion, they formed their small colonies all over the world, and in the centre of most of them there soon appeared an Orthodox parish with a priest supported by the voluntary contributions of the people, who were often destitute and homesick. The intelligentsia had begun rediscovering their Church at the beginning of the twentieth century, a process which was continued in exile and greatly assisted by the presence among the emigrants of several outstanding Christian thinkers, such as Fr. Sergei Bulgakov (b. 1871–1944), Nikolai Berdyaev (d. 1948), Nikolai Losski (b. 1870), and Fr. Vassili Zenkovski. Soon new names were added to their ranks, of men and women who acquired their reputation as Christian scholars after they were obliged to start life abroad. Among these are Bp. Kassian Bezobrasov (b. 1892), Fr. George Florovski (b. 1893), George Fedotov, Lev Zander (b. 1893), Nadezhda Gorodetski, Metr. Anthony (b. 1914). Two distinguished Western theologians who have entered into communion with the Orthodox Church, Fr. Alexis van der Mensbrugghe (b. 1899) and Fr.

Lev Gillet (*b.* 1893), have also greatly contributed to the better understanding between Russian and Western Christians.[1] Several well-known bishops left Russia with their flocks; among them were the Metropolitan of Kiev, Antoni Khrapovitski (*d.* 1936), the Metropolitan Eulogi of Volhynia, and Archbishop Anastasi of Kishenev (Bessarabia).

The great political upheaval which forced all these people to leave their own country and the fierce attack on the Russian Church which accompanied it profoundly stirred both the leaders and the rank and file, and in 1921 the first Council representing the Russian Church in exile met in Karlovtsi in Jugoslavia. It consisted of twelve bishops and eighty representatives of the clergy and laity, some elected and some co-opted, and gathered from all corners of Europe. The contrast between the quiet of a small provincial town and the high tension of this gathering was striking. The centre of everybody's attention was the suffering of the Christians in Russia, and the ways in which the Church in Exile could help them. The civil war was still fresh in the minds of most of the members of the Council, and few of them thought that the Soviet Government would survive for long. A considerable group of the laity, headed by the Metropolitan Antoni, believed that it was the duty of the Church to assist the nation in the process of political reconstruction, which they associated with the restoration of the monarchy. Another group of members of the Council, led by the Metropolitan Eulogi, were opposed to the association of the Church with any definite political programme, and considered that the Church must unite people of different political outlooks. The Council was unable to reconcile these two points of view, and, although an open breach was avoided, it became clear that the Russian Church in exile had failed to devise a policy acceptable to all.[2] The Council of 1921, in spite of the opposition of a strong minority, adopted a resolution in which the restoration of the monarchy was advocated. This action still further aggravated the difficult position of the Church in Russia, and in 1923 the Patriarch Tikhon officially dissociated himself from the organs of ecclesiastical government created by the Karlovtsi Council and ordered them to be closed down.

[1] See N. Zernov, *Russian Emigré Authors: A Biographical Index and Bibliography of Their Works, 1921–1972*, Boston, 1973.
[2] See N. Zernov, " The Schism Within the Russian Church in Diaspora ", *Eastern Churches Review*, 1st part, vol. vii, no. 1, 1975; 2nd part, vol. vii, no. 2, 1975.

The condemnation brought about a split in the ranks of the Russian Church in exile. The Metropolitan Eulogi accepted Tikhon's decision, and the majority of clergy and people in France and other Western European countries followed his lead. But the Metropolitan Antoni declared that the Patriarch's decision had been forced upon him by the pressure of the anti-Christian Government, and he remained at the head of the so-called Karlovtsi Synod. The scattered Russian congregations in the Balkans, the Church in the Far East, and a minority in Western Europe accepted his point of view. In 1927 the Metropolitan Sergius, who became in that year a vice-guardian of the vacant Patriarchal Throne, issued an appeal to all Russian Christians abroad asking them to declare their loyalty to the Soviet State, if they wished to retain their link with the Church in Russia. This appeal affected only the Metropolitan Eulogi and his parishes, for the Karlovtsi party had already broken away from the Church inside the U.S.S.R. The majority of Russians were unwilling to accept the Metropolitan Sergius's request, for they were no longer citizens of the U.S.S.R. The Metropolitan Eulogi, supported by the Council of clergy and laity which met in Paris in 1931, asked the Patriarch of Constantinople to take him and his diocese under his jurisdiction. This request was granted, but a few parishes, led by Bishop Veniamin, preferred to remain attached to Moscow and formed their own organisation.

This situation lasted till the end of the Second World War, when the Patriarch Alexis invited the Russian Church in exile to return under his jurisdiction. The Metropolitan Eulogi availed himself of this offer and in 1945 was solemnly received back by the Metropolitan Nicolas, who came specially to Paris. This action was however criticised by a considerable number of clergy and laity, and after the death of the Metropolitan Eulogi, the majority of his parishes reaffirmed their desire to remain under Constantinople.

This means that the Russian Church abroad while remaining united in faith and worship, is divided into three jurisdictions, each of which reflects a different attitude to the tension between the godless state and the Church in the U.S.S.R.

Those Russians who follow the Metropolitan Philaret, the successor to the Metropolitan Antoni, reject the possibility of any agreement between the Communists and the Christians, and consider themselves to be the only right spokesmen of the Russian

Church. Those who adhere to the jurisdiction of Constantinople feel unable either to support or to condemn the policy pursued by the Moscow hierarchy. The rest trust and are ready to obey it.

These three tendencies have a greater importance than may appear at first sight, for they are more than mere disputes among the Russians in exile. They also reflect the existence of different currents of thought among the Christians in the U.S.S.R. There, too, the members of the Church have taken a different attitude to the godless State, some being uncompromisingly opposed to it, others ready to collaborate with it in different degrees in politics and in social action, as long as their allegiance to Christianity is not challenged. Under the present conditions of strict Communist censorship it is impossible to form any accurate estimate of the exact position and comparative strength of these groups, but it is necessary to remember their existence whenever any attempt is made to describe the reaction of the Russian Christians to the Communist experiment.

The other serious task which confronted the Russian Church in Exile concerned relations with Western Christians, and each of the above-mentioned parties chose its own line of dealing with it. The members of the Karlovtsi Synod, with few exceptions, were suspicious of the Western world. They felt bitterly that the fierce conflict between Christians and atheists in Russia had created abroad little sympathy for the Russian Church, and they were convinced that this lack of charity and understanding was the consequence of the grave defects in doctrine from which the Roman and Reformed Churches alike suffered. The Metropolitan Antoni, himself the most able theologian of that group, was outspokenly anti-Western in his sentiments and outlook. The section of the Church under the jurisdiction of the Moscow Patriarch became interested in the establishment of closer contacts with the Western Christians only after the end of the Second World War and as a result of the change in the policy of the centre. This task therefore fell chiefly upon the Christians who followed the Metropolitan Eulogi. These included most of the theologians of the Russian Church and, owing to their initiative, several important Christian institutions sprang up among the Russians in exile. These were the Russian Student Christian Movement, started in 1923, and the Theological College, founded in Paris in 1925. Closely associated with them was " the Y.M.C.A. Press ", sponsored by the American

Y.M.C.A., but directed by Russian theologians including Prof. Nikolai Berdyaev. These three channels helped the Russian Church abroad to express its mind on the major issues of the present crisis and also to establish a friendly contact with the Christians of the West. These were almost the first contacts it had made since the beginning of its history.[1]

The Russian Student Christian Movement was the pioneer in this field. It came into existence in the form of scattered Christian Study Circles in the different capitals in Europe. The American Y.M.C.A. and the World Student Christian Federation helped their representatives to meet at a Conference in Pšerov in Czechoslovakia in September 1923. Most of these delegates had little knowledge of Western Christians, and they looked down on them as seriously deficient in true religion. They were, however, soon convinced that they had much more in common with the Christian Students of Europe and America than they had thought, and friendly relations were established which helped the Russians to enter into the life of the Western Christians and share with them their religious experience. Especially fruitful was the co-operation with the members of the Anglican Communion, who, as the Russians discovered to their surprise, stood nearer to them than the representatives of any other Western tradition. In 1927, a conference between the Eastern Orthodox and the Christians of Great Britain was held at St. Albans in England, under the auspices of the Russian and British Student Christian Movements. The particular feature of its programme was the placing of the Eucharist in the centre of its work. The Orthodox and the Anglican Communion Services were celebrated on alternate days, and the members of the Conference were present at both, though they were not in Communion with one another. The Conference was attended by distinguished British and Russian theologians, including Bishop Gore and the Rev. Prof. S. Bulgakov. It was a great success, and, when its members met again in the following year, they decided to cement their unity in Christ by founding the Fellowship of St. Alban and St. Sergius, Bishop Walter Frere, C.R., being elected its first President. Since 1928, this

---

[1] This book deals only with the Russians, therefore this chapter does not mention those Western Christians including several outstanding Anglicans (like John Birkbeck (*d.* 1917) for instance) who made special study of the Russian Church, and have greatly contributed to the establishment of a better understanding between the Orthodox and Western Christians.

society has become an important unofficial channel for the relations between Orthodox and Western Christians[1]. Its conferences, camps and publications have inaugurated a new stage in their co-operation, based on mutual trust and full realisation that both sides can learn from and teach the other. The spirit of genuine friendship and mutual respect was the fruit of Eucharistic unity, experienced by the members of this Fellowship. Their influence soon spread in the wider sphere of œcumenical work. Owing to the initiative of the Fellowship members, the World Conference held in 1939 in Amsterdam was the first to include in its official programme celebrations of the Eucharist according to the different traditions. The Russians maintained that the act of worship instituted by Christ Himself ought not to be excluded from the gathering of those who wanted to obey the Will of their Saviour.

The active participation of the Russian Orthodox in all the theological, social and œcumenical activities of Western Christians during the last fifty years has been a revelation to both sides. They have realised that in spite of centuries of isolation and hostility, they agree in the fundamentals of the Faith, and that their differences usually represent complementary aspects of their approach to Christian religion. Where Eastern Christians are strong, their Western brothers are often defective; but where the latter can show solid achievements, the Orthodox lag behind, and need advice and help. This is equally applicable to the realm of theological thought and to the Church's social action. The new books produced by the Russian theologians in exile bear witness to this truth. They have incorporated many results of Western scholarship and Christian experience, whilst, on the other hand, they have themselves proved stimulating both to Roman Catholic and to Protestant writers and readers.

The wall of partition which has for so long kept Russian Christians from contact with the rest of Christendom has at last been breached. The Church of Christ has been enriched and strengthened thereby, and its members are now better equipped for their common task of bringing back to Christ a world which has deserted its true Master.

[1] A pamphlet describing the work of the Fellowship can be obtained from St. Basil's House, 52 Ladbroke Grove, London, W11 2PB.

CHAPTER XX

THE MESSAGE OF THE RUSSIAN CHURCH

THE history of Russia is the story of a lonely nation. From the
time of their conversion to Christianity in the tenth century
until the present day, its people have lived in almost complete
spiritual isolation, and only on rare occasions have they shared
their experience with the rest of the world. Yet the Russians
inhabit the land which forms a natural bridge between Europe
and Asia; their country has been constantly menaced on both
flanks, and they have many a time endured the assaults of their
neighbours. Such trials and suffering from hostility have driven
them all through their history to search for ways of reconciliation
between East and West—a difficult task they have felt themselves
chosen to fulfil. The sharp turning-points in their cultural development, its rifts, tensions and revolutions, the removal of the
capital from Kiev to Moscow, from Moscow to St. Petersburg and
back again to Moscow—all these events have their origin in a
desire to find the balance between the conflicting outlooks of
Europe and Asia, between Western claims to personal freedom and
Oriental insistence on the integration of the individual into the
community.

In spite of their centuries-long separation, the Russians have
always thought of their country as an integral part of Christendom, and they have firmly believed that a leading rôle is
assigned to them in the history of mankind. The land they
inhabit, the history through which they have passed and the
religion they have chosen make them a nation with a unique
outlook and culture.

The Russian attitude to life is marked by a conception of the
Universe as one and undivided, and by strong sense of the
mutual dependence of all men. This outlook is the natural
response to the influence of the great Russian Plain with its
boundless spaces. Russian scenery has the qualities of the ocean.
Like the sea, it is dominated by the vault of heaven, and this
makes man conscious of eternity and of a world wider than
earth itself.

A Russian does not divide life into compartments. Classi-

176

fications and subdivisions, so characteristic of the European mind, do not appeal to him. He thinks and feels along the broad lines of the general and the universal. He is more interested in the final goal than in the immediate task confronting him; he is not satisfied with the temporal expedient, but searches for the absolute and wants to know the whole truth; he is impatient of limited objectives and fascinated by ideas which have a world-wide application.

This universalism is coupled with a recognition of the interdependence of all human beings. On Russia's open, unprotected plain an individual often feels lost and helpless; only by working with others can he achieve his aim and avoid manifold dangers. As there are no geographical barriers in Russia, so there are no distinct boundaries and antagonisms. All those races that inhabit the vast land form one body, mixing freely with one another and recognising their common destiny. This bond of unity is strong because the largest of these nations, the Russians proper, have behaved initially more as equals than as rulers in regard to the other smaller and weaker nationalities.[1]

A third characteristic is the humility of the people, the source of their physical endurance and moral strength. Humility means realism—the frank recognition of one's limitations and achievements. It was the Mongol invasion of the thirteenth century which taught the nation humility and changed a self-willed and undisciplined people into builders of a great Empire. The Tartar domination, which lasted for 200 years, cured the Russians of arrogance. Nations which have for centuries experienced suffering and frustration as the helpless victims of aggressive conquerors cannot themselves enjoy the sight of an enemy prostrate at their feet, nor boast of being a master race. This is well illustrated in General Alexander Suvorov's famous charge to his troops, which expressed a readiness to forgive—this typically Russian virtue. His order contains the following words: " The enemy has surrendered. . . . Shew mercy to him. Be kind to the prisoners. A soldier is not a bandit. It is a sin to kill when this can be avoided. Our enemies are men as we are. Overcome the foe with magnanimity."[2]

Freedom from national pride and mercy to the defeated

---

[1] The policy of the Empire during its decline broke away disastrously from this tradition.

[2] Leninism stands in sharpest contrast to this spirit.

have made the Russians sensitive to the influence of the other inhabitants of their land.   A Russian does not feel it beneath his dignity to adopt the manners and to learn the language of his neighbours, even if they are under his rule.   In the Caucasus he wears the dress of the natives, and in Siberia he follows the customs of the Finnish and Mongolian tribes and speaks their dialects.   This adaptability has helped to make the Russians successful colonisers and has enabled them to cement the unity of their realm without destroying the individual cultures of its non-Russian minorities.

Such are the marks left by history and geography upon the outlook of the Russian people.   But the greatest influence in the formation of their character was that of their Church—the least institutional and the most cosmic among the great national Churches of the modern world.   The Church has taught the Russians the art of Christian living, revealed to them the mystery of the Incarnation, and provided them with a pattern of a social order (*sobornost*) which aims at reconciling the Western assertion of man's independence with the Eastern desire for fellowship. The Orthodox Church has been the tutor of the Russians, and to the nature of its instruction they owe their chief characteristics, their strength and their weakness.   It is remarkable that, in the fulfilment of its main task of teaching the Russians the truth of divine victory over evil revealed in the Resurrection, the Church has been powerfully supported by the lessons given to the nation by nature and history.

Every spring a Russian witnesses the resurrection of Nature. After six months of immobility and death, life comes back to the Russian land.   With noise and triumph, the rivers and lakes burst the ice which has kept them imprisoned for half a year. Grass and flowers appear over-night in the fields, which for many months have been covered with a thick white mantle; the birds begin to sing; the air becomes scented; men and animals feel exhilarated and reborn.   Life proves once more to be stronger than death.   This yearly experience of the resurrection of Nature has a striking parallel in the history of the Russian people, for, as a nation, they, too, were weighed down, deprived of freedom, overwhelmed for two centuries by the Mongol invader.   Then a spring day came; the nation burst its heavy chains and returned to life and light.   And this resurrection was achieved by the spiritual force of Christian faith which was mightier than the military skill and numerical strength of the Tartars.

This power of resurrection in Nature and history assumed for the Russians its full meaning in the light of Christ's victory over sin and death, and therefore Easter is celebrated by them with a joy and splendour unequalled in any other Church. In Russia, not a few devout people only, but the nation as a body has for centuries praised and thanked God for Christ's Rising from the tomb. The service on Easter night is an experience which has no parallel in the worship of other nations. Only those who have been present at this service can realise all that the Resurrection means to the Russian people.

Universalism, interdependence, sobriety, and belief in resurrection are the four corner-stones of Russian culture, and the view of life presented thereby explains how it is that the Russians feel different from the rest of Christendom, and why they themselves described their distinct contribution under the curious name of " Moscow, the Third and Last Rome ".

When, for the first time, the conviction of their mission dawned upon the people, there was a good deal of naïve self-satisfaction, which has for a long time obscured the understanding of their true calling. But the gradual unfolding of history has not discredited this prophecy; on the contrary, this has been enlarged, strengthened and confirmed.

The teaching that Moscow is the Third Rome implies belief that there are three distinct stages in the evolution of the Church. The first one is associated with the old Rome, the ancient seat of Paternal Authority. Rome stands for unity, discipline and order; it emphasises the oneness of the Church; it is rigid and demands obedience; it is practical and mistrusts intellectual freedom. It reveals to mankind the Fatherhood of God.

The second stage is associated with Constantinople; with the intellectual approach to religion; with definitions of dogmas and the controversies unavoidable in the pursuit of this task. The second Rome reveals the Second Person of the Trinity— the Logos. It excels in the dialectic process, in the discovery of truth through reason, in asserting the harmony between human and divine. This aspect of Christianity suffered a grievous blow at the time of the fall of Constantinople, but the line of development interrupted in the East was resumed under a new form in the West by those Christians who embraced the Reformation.

For intellectually the Protestants continued the work started by the Byzantine theologians, and they displayed the same mental keenness, and the same mistrust of the old Rome as was shown by her Eastern opponents.

The third stage in Church history is connected with Moscow, the least legalistic of all the great centres of Christendom. Moscow stands for the unsurpassed beauty and glory of worship. She believes that the whole of life is the sphere of the operation of divine Grace and is primarily concerned with the application of Christianity to communal life. Her Church represents the most devotional and the most artistic of all Christian traditions. She praises the Holy Ghost, the Spirit of Truth and Giver of Life.

The Russian Church used to be deficient in discipline and organisation; inarticulate in speech and logical thought, but captivated by the vision of the transfigured cosmos; confident of the resurrection of the dead, and expectant of the Second Coming. Russian Christians have never passed through the invigorating but also formal school of Latin grammar and Greek thought. They lost much, but they have gained much. Looking upon the world with eyes that had never seen the glorious monuments of classical civilisation, they had no temptation to copy them. They moved along their own road and reached conclusions which correct and complete the all-important findings made by other Churches. Many of the facts known to the Russians have escaped the notice of the better-trained but also more rational Western Christians. The Russians have penetrated into secrets of human life hidden from others. They heard the call of the Holy Spirit in a way unfamiliar to the rest of the Christian world. When, at length, their discoveries were conveyed to the West through the writings of Dostoevsky, Soloviev, Berdyaev, and other modern authors, they revolutionised many accepted Western notions and broadened both the Roman and the Protestant outlook.

In some respects the spirit of Russian Christianity is Judaic, for it conceives of religion neither as a well-organised institution, nor as a system of doctrines, but as a rule of life, which affects every detail of the daily order—food, dress, manners. This is because Christianity is, for the Russian, the power that transforms the Universe into God's manifest Kingdom, and at its centre stands the Holy Eucharist. This most sacred rite brings matter, through the medium of man's faith, love and prayer, into the fullness of communion with the Holy Spirit. The material world is not destroyed, but purified, regenerated, made into a vehicle of Divine Grace and elevated into the realm of life eternal. The coming resurrection of all men and the transfiguration of the cosmos are reaffirmed at each Eucharist, and those who partake of its mystery pledge themselves to be God's collaborators in the fulfilment of the purpose for which He has created the world. Such is the message of the Third and Last Rome; such is the task of the Church as seen by the Saints and Prophets of Russia.

It is not by accident that this primarily Eucharistic and Cosmic Church has been made the object of the fiercest attack of modern secularism and atheism. Russian Christians in the twentieth century formed a nation-wide worshipping community instead of being, like many other Churches, reduced to the status of a denomination. Their entire life was still influenced by belief in the Incarnation, and all their daily customs and traditions expressed faith in the Holy Trinity and in the redemption of the whole world. The leaders of the godless movement well understood the intimate connection between religion and home life in Russia, and they struck hard at the customs of the people, altering their days of rest and work, forbidding the meals associated with Christian festivals, interfering with marriage, with the upbringing of children and with the burial of the dead. The fight against God was not an abstract, ideological struggle in Russia. God was in the very centre of daily life; no one could remain neutral; everybody had to side with God or against Him, and on this choice depended everything—man's ideas of good and evil, his manners, speech and even his food. The strength of the early Communists was in the integral nature of their doctrine: they claimed to know the whole truth and they demanded unconditional allegiance from every man. But they met an all-embracing type of Christianity which did not accept division between secular and sacred, which believed that the whole earth must be transformed through man into the temple of the Holy Spirit.

Militant atheism, equipped with the most up-to-date modern weapons—wireless, propaganda, press, schools, and concentration camps—tried to smash the resistance of the Christians, who were unsupported by any power other than the grace of the Holy Spirit. Lenin, Trotsky, Zinoviev and other early leaders of the

Communist Party were determined to create a new order. They pursued a policy of the most aggressive Westernisation, erased the very name of Russia, banned the national history from schools, re-named the ancient cities and systematically destroyed historical monuments. The Communist attempt to uproot Russia from her Christian past was accompanied by an equally relentless assault on all Westernised classes, especially on the radical intelligentsia. Lenin treated with the same hostility western democracy and Russian Orthodoxy. His totalitarianism had been founded on propaganda, deception, fear and oppression. Atheism and materi-alism, which had been presented by the Communists as liberating forces, provided a justification for the unprecedented enslavement of man and his cruel degradation. The Russian people have been more isolated than ever before. At the same time their sense of mission has been exploited and distorted; the unnatural and ex-plosive mixture of patriotism and international Marxism has made Russia a threat to the rest of mankind.

A mighty hurricane has blown over Russia during these fateful decades; many venerable traditions, cherished ideas and age-long customs have been irrevocably swept away. Little has remained undestroyed, but among these few imperishable values stands, as on solid rock, the Orthodox Church with its vision of *Sobornost*. This ideal of " togetherness in freedom ", founded on Christian fellow-ship, has always been the main driving force behind all the social and political endeavours of Russian people. Their history reveals its proper meaning only if it is seen as the expression of the desire to treat their rapidly expanding state as one big family. The Chris-tians in Russia today are still deprived of freedom of speech, but the underground voices (*Samizdat*) which reach the West unmistakably witness that they have not forsaken their traditional aspirations; persecution has purified their conception of *Sobornost* and their sense of mission.

Emerging from their torment they, with the rest of mankind, will have to meet the new challenge of modern de-christianised civilisation. They will have to face the uncontrolled developments of technology and science, and the increasing belief in the power of coercion manifested in Marxism, fascism, nationalism and terror-ism. All these are variations of that heresy, as old as the history of fallen man, which teaches that man is his own master and that the satisfaction of his material appetites is the main purpose of his existence. Christianity is the only power that fully reveals the supremacy of love, freedom and life over hatred, slavery and destruction.

The divided Christians are everywhere in retreat, but the growing awareness of the urgency of their reconciliation gives hope that the battle for survival has not been lost. Only together, united by faith and charity, can the Christian Community face the challenge of the modern world. In this quest for unity the experience of Russians makes an essential contribution. Humiliated, they were not conquered. Abandoning their self-sufficiency, they should now be better prepared to share with others their gifts. The message of the Russian Church still is that Christians must trust and obey the Holy Spirit, " the Comforter, the Giver of Life ", the source of unity and freedom.

BIBLIOGRAPHY

General Introduction to the Eastern Orthodox Church

Bulgakov, S., *The Orthodox Church*. London 1935.
Ware, T. (Archimandrite Kallistos), *The Orthodox Church*. London 1975.
Zernov, N., *Eastern Christendom*. London 1961.

General Introduction to the Character of the Russian People

Baring, M., *The Russian People*. London 1914.
Lawrence, J., *Russia in the Making*. London 1954.
Weidle, W., *Russia Absent and Present*. London 1952.
Williams, H., *Russia and the Russians*. London 1914.

General Surveys of Russian Church History

Frere, W. H., *Some Links in the Chain of Russian Church History*. London 1918.
Zernov, N., *Moscow the Third Rome*. London 1944.

The Great Schism in the Russian Church

Avvacum, *The Life of Archpriest Avvacum, by himself*. London 1924.
Palmer, W., *The Patriarch and the Tsar*. 6 vols. London 1871–6.

Contemporary Russian Theology

A Bulgakov Anthology, ed. N. Zernov and J. Pain. London and Philadelphia 1976.
Florovsky, G., *Collected Works*. 3 vols. Belmont, Mass. 1972–6.
Khomiakov, A., *The Church is One*. London 1948.
Schmemann, A., *Ultimate Questions: An Anthology of Modern Russian Religious Thought*. New York 1965.
Soloviev, V., *The Justification of the Good*. London 1918.

Russian Orthodox Spirituality

Anon., *The Way of a Pilgrim* and *The Pilgrim Continues his Way*, tr. R. M. French. London 1954.
Anthony, Archbishop, *School for Prayer*. London 1971.
— *Living Prayer*. London 1966.
Elchaninov, A., *The Diary of a Russian Priest*. London 1976.
Fedotov, G., *A Treasury of Russian Spirituality*. London 1950.
— *The Russian Religious Mind*. 2 vols. London 1966–7.
Gorodetsky, N., *The Humiliated Christ in Modern Russian Thought*. London 1938.

John of Kronstadt, *Select Passages from My Life in Christ*, ed. W. J. Grisbrooke. London 1966.
Lossky, V., *The Mystical Theology of the Eastern Church*. Greenwood, South Carolina, 1968.
Pascal, P., *The Religion of the Russian People*. New York 1934.
Sofrony, Archimandrite, *The Undistorted Image: Staretz Silouan (1866–1938)*. London 1952.

Russian Saints

Amvrosy of Optina, J. B. Dunlop. Belmont, Mass. 1972.
St. Seraphim of Sarov: *Flame in the Snow*, J. de Beausobre. London 1945.
St. Seraphim of Sarov, V. Zander. London 1975.
St. Sergius of Radonezh: *St. Sergius and Russian Spirituality*, P. Kovalevsky. New York n.d.
St. Sergius, Builder of Russia, N. Zernov. London 1939.
St. Tikhon of Zadonsk, N. Gorodetsky. London and New York 1951.

Russian Orthodox Worship

Gogol, N., *The Divine Liturgy*. London 1960.
A Manual of Eastern Orthodox Prayers. London 1962.
The Orthodox Liturgy. London 1968.

Russian Religious Art and Architecture

Hamilton, G., *The Art and Architecture of Russia*. Pelican History of Art. London 1954.
Lazarev, V., *Old Russian Murals and Mosaics*. London 1966.
Ouspensky, L. and Lossky, V., *The Meaning of Icons*. London 1947.

Russian Orthodoxy and Communism

Berdyaev, N., *The Russian Revolution*. London 1931.
Stepun, T., *The Russian Soul and Revolution*. London 1936.

The Russian Church under Communist Rule

Beeson, T., *Discretion and Valour*. London 1974.
Bourdeaux, M., *Patriarch and Prophets: Persecution of the Russian Church Today*. London 1970.
Fletcher, W. C., *Nikolai* (Metropolitan Nikolai of Krutitskii). New York 1968.
Kolarz, W., *Religion in the Soviet Union*. London 1961.
Struve, N., *Christians in Contemporary Russia*. London 1967.

The Russian Church and the Christian West

Birkbeck, J., *Russia and the English Church*. London 1895.

Newman, Cardinal, *A Visit to the Russian Church*. London 1882.

Waddams, H., *Anglo-Russian Theological Conference, Moscow, July 1956*. London 1958.

Zander, L., *Vision and Action*. London 1952.

Zernov, N., *The Reintegration of the Church*. London 1952.

— *Orthodox Encounter*. London 1961.

— *The Russian Religious Renaissance of the Twentieth Century*. London 1963.

INDEX OF PERSONS